Variations on
WAYNE SLEEP

Photographs by Chris Nash

HEINEMANN : LONDON

Variations on WAYNE SLEEP

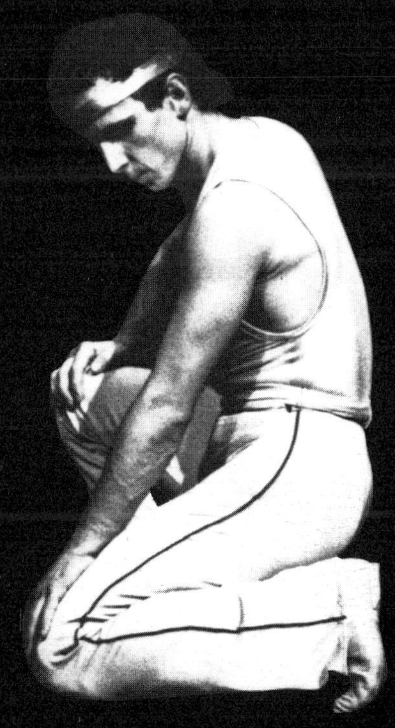

Designed and picture-edited by Craig Dodd

William Heinemann Ltd
10 Upper Grosvenor Street, London W1X 9PA

LONDON MELBOURNE TORONTO
JOHANNESBURG AUCKLAND

First published 1983
Text © Gravity Productions Ltd. and Gay Search 1983
Photographs © Chris Nash 1983
~~434 70756 2~~ 434 70755 4
Filmset and printed in Great Britain by
BAS Printers Limited, Over Wallop, Hampshire

CONTENTS

Cast of Characters

Wayne Sleep   Star of 'Variations'
Marti Webb   Star of 'Tell Me on a Sunday'

The Dancers

Linda-Mae Brewer (known as just 'Linda')
Jane Darling
Andrea Durant
Linda Gibbs

Claude-Paul Henry (known as just 'Paul')
Andy Norman
Sandy Strallen
Paul Tomkinson

Understudies

Angela Robinson
Stewart Arnold

Andrew Lloyd Webber	Composer and Co-producer
John Caird	Director
Cameron Mackintosh	Co-producer
Anthony van Laast	Choreographer
Sue Hywel	Assistant Choreographer/Ballet Mistress
David Hersey	Designer
Robin Don	Costume Designer
Anne Sinclair	Costume Supervisor
Bob West	Company Manager
Mike Halford	Deputy Stage Manager
Gill van Zwanenberg	Assistant Stage Manager
Harry Rabinowitz	Musical Supervisor
Robert Purvis	Rehearsal Pianist

When we embarked on *Song and Dance* early in 1982, I had no idea what the audience reaction would be. No one had ever put on a 'concert for the theatre' before, and certainly no one had successfully presented a forty-five minute dance piece in a West End theatre.

I am, of course, absolutely delighted that the show has been such a huge success, with wonderful audience response night after night. It is exhilarating to be part of all this, but perhaps what the audience isn't aware of is just how a dance piece like *Variations* is put together.

I hope this book will show you what it's like to be a dancer involved in the building of a new production – all the pain you have to go through, all the different possibilities you have to explore and reject – before you end up with what looks like a comparatively simple forty-five minute dance piece.

We started out with a piece of music, Andrew Lloyd Webber's 'Variations', and the desire to create a dance piece that had a theme, as the music does, and wasn't just a series of unconnected dances, which the general, theatre-going public would enjoy. This book follows our progress from that day, through the six weeks of rehearsals to the opening night.

Wayne Sleep

PRELUDE

Wayne Sleep is one of the most outstanding and talented male dancers in Britain today. Born in Plymouth, he started dancing almost as soon as he could walk, and at twelve, won a Leverhulme Scholarship to the Royal Ballet School. He joined the Royal Ballet Company, becoming a Principal Dancer in 1973.

Though his size precluded him from many of the leading roles, his irreverent personality, Puckish sense of humour and phenomenal ability to jump and spin enabled him to turn cameo parts, like Hop o' my Thumb in *The Sleeping Beauty*, the leader of the mandoline dancers in *Romeo and Juliet*, and many others specially created for him by choreographers like Sir Frederick Ashton, Dame Ninette de Valois and Kenneth Macmillan, into regularly show-stopping roles.

In the mid-seventies, he began to stretch his talent, dancing and singing in West End shows like *The Point*, and *Aladdin* with Danny La Rue at the Palladium, and most recently, in the award-winning *Cats*.

As a choreographer, his work has included *The Point, David and Goliath* (with Robert North for London Contemporary Dance Theatre), *Adam's Rib*, a jazz ballet for BBC Television, and the dance sequences for the film *Death on the Nile*.

He has also played straight dramatic roles like Ariel in *The Tempest* at Regents Park Open Air Theatre, Tony Lumpkin in *She Stoops to Conquer* and cameo film roles in *The Virgin Soldiers* and *The First Great Train Robbery*. He has appeared in numerous television programmes from variety shows in which he has sung and danced, to classical works like Stravinsky's *The Soldier's Tale*, and his sparky, engaging personality has made him a very popular chat show guest.

Although he is now a versatile all-round performer, dance obviously remains central to his life and so, in 1980, Wayne Sleep decided to form his own dance company, Dash, and put together a stage show which would be quite unlike anything seen in Britain before.

What Wayne wanted was a vehicle in which he could perform ballet, jazz, contemporary and tap all in the same evening's programme because he didn't see why each style of dance had to be slotted into a different compartment. As it was, he found himself having to move from theatre to theatre – the Royal Opera House for ballet, the West End for variety, cabaret and television for tap and the impressions of people like Robin Cousins and Bette Midler he has begun doing recently.

Dash, he hoped, would give him the freedom to include the best of all styles of dance in one evening and to go straight from a crazy routine into a classical *pas de deux*.

Wayne had already worked out a programme for the first Dash show, using music by a range of composers, from Tchaikovsky to Scott Joplin, but, thinking ahead, he had begun searching for a single piece of music to which he could choreograph a whole second half. He considered albums by groups like Pink Floyd, but found them too self-indulgent and lacking the variety he was looking for to sustain fifty minutes of *all* styles of dance. Then he heard Andrew Lloyd Webber's 'Variations', and he knew he had found what he was looking for.

The 'Variations' in question, on Paganini's famous A Minor Caprice No. 24, had been composed in 1977 by Andrew Lloyd Webber for his cellist brother Julian. The result was a hit album, released in 1978, from which Melvyn Bragg took the signature tune for London Weekend Television's 'South Bank Show'. Not long after he had heard 'Variations', Wayne met Andrew at a party and mentioned the idea of choreographing a dance piece to it. Andrew seemed very interested and thought it might make a second half to something else he had done – a musical setting of some poems from T. S. Eliot's *Old Possum's Book of Practical Cats*. It had been well-received at his own private festival, but he didn't feel it would make a whole evening in the theatre by itself. But then Eliot's widow, Valerie, gave him some previously unpublished cat poems, and *Cats* no longer needed a second half.

Wayne was invited to star in *Cats*, but before rehearsals began, he took Dash on a very successful tour of Britain and 'Variations' was shelved for the time being.

In May 1981 *Cats* opened at the New London Theatre to marvellous reviews and soon became the most popular show in the West End, booked solid for months ahead.

With two hit musicals running in the West End (*Evita* was still playing to full houses), Andrew turned his attention to 'Tell Me on a Sunday', the one-woman song cycle he had written with Don Black for Marti Webb in 1979. It had been a very successful album, and the television show had been so well received that it was repeated, by popular demand, less than four weeks later.

In 1981, Andrew and Don Black began exploring ways of presenting 'Tell Me on a Sunday', with Marti Webb, in the theatre. They were discussing it with Cameron Mackintosh, co-producer of *Cats*, when Wayne revived the idea of choreographing 'Variations', and it was Cameron Mackintosh who had the bright idea of putting them together as *Song and Dance*. Since it was going to be unlike anything ever presented in the West End before, they decided to add the subtitle 'A Concert for the Theatre'.

Wayne was committed to *Cats*, until mid-January 1982 and would need a holiday before starting work on the new show, so *Song and Dance* could not open before late March at a theatre yet to be decided. Rehearsals would start six weeks earlier, in mid-February.

Andrew invited John Caird, a director with the Royal Shakespeare Company, to direct the show. Although his experience was exclusively in straight theatre (he was Trevor Nunn's co-director on the award-winning *Nicholas Nickleby*), he is no mean musician himself and is extremely interested in musical theatre.

While he was to be responsible for the overall concept of both halves, obviously for 'Variations' the choice of choreographer was critical. Although Wayne has choreographed a number of pieces for the stage and for television, there was never any question in his mind that he might do it himself.

'I couldn't choreograph anything longer than a three minute solo for myself, and so forty-five minutes was out of the question. The problem is you give yourself steps that you think are interesting, but they don't necessarily look good on you. Obviously, I wanted to be closely involved in the evolution of the choreography, but I'd have enough to think about, just giving a performance, without having to worry about everything else as well!'

Wayne's first thoughts were to approach an American choreographer, like Bob Fosse, or Jerome Robbins, but Andrew, with his passionate interest in fostering the English musical, suggested they use an English choreographer. 'I think he's right. Choreographers haven't been encouraged to develop in this country – all the work is given to one or two people, so that nobody up-and-coming gets a look-in. Most new choreographers have to go into television where all they're asked to do is provide moving wallpaper for singers, which really doesn't allow them to show their talent.

'I did know of one choreographer who was doing interesting work – Anthony van Laast. I'd worked with him years ago at the London

Contemporary Dance Theatre when, ironically, he danced in a ballet I'd choreographed. I knew he'd left and gone into the commercial world as a choreographer. He'd done lots of TV shows and films, and also Kate Bush's stage show which I hadn't seen, but which I'd heard was full of good ideas, which is what you need for a forty-five minute piece. If you've got the ideas, the steps take care of themselves. Anyway, I thought that with his background in contemporary and jazz dance, and his understanding of the classical body, he'd be able to do all the different styles of dance we wanted.'

Anthony van Laast was approached and leapt at the chance and embarked on a series of meetings with Andrew Lloyd Webber, John Caird and Wayne to decide what the theme of 'Variations' should be.

The first idea was the life story of Paganini, the composer, with Wayne playing the Maestro, but this was soon abandoned because, having read all the biographies, everyone agreed there was little in his life – apart from his music and his affairs – on which to base a ballet.

So they had to think again. Anthony had rejected the idea of relationships early on because all it suggested to him was an endless series of *pas de deux*. But when John Caird came up with a more detailed scenario about relationships *now*, it seemed the best solution. Since the first half 'Tell Me on a Sunday', explored one woman's relationships, it meant that the audience would see the same theme explored in two completely different ways, in two different disciplines.

There was some discussion early on about linking the two halves by making Wayne the third or fourth man in Marti's life, and by having a dancing clone of Marti in the second half, but that was dismissed quite quickly as too heavy-handed.

Wayne felt very strongly that the two halves should NOT be linked in any way, but he was happy with the relationships theme. 'It's a big enough concept to base a ballet on, complex enough to provide lots of variety, but simple enough for audiences to grasp. In dance, simple ideas are the best.'

Since 'Variations' was to be a showcase for dancers, Wayne and Anthony set about finding the best soloists in each style of dance, jazz, contemporary, ballet and tap, who would also be able to dance in the other styles. There were to be four girls and four boys in addition to Wayne.

Some of the dancers selected themselves. Jane Darling, probably the best jazz dancer in the country, had known Wayne for years, and was a founder member of Dash, as was Linda Brewer, a twenty-year-old Australian who is a brilliant tap dancer. Wayne and Anthony both knew and admired Linda Gibbs, principal dancer with the London Contemporary Dance Theatre, and Wayne had been at the Royal Ballet School with Andrea Durant, former principal dancer with the Scottish Ballet.

As for the boys, Paul Henry had been a student of Anthony's for years. Wayne had worked briefly with Paul Tomkinson, though at the time, he didn't know that Paul had been a member of the British Junior Gymnastics squad, and was a marvellous acrobat. Sue Hywel, Anthony's assistant, recommended Andy Norman, who had danced in a number of ballet companies and West End musicals. Sandy Strallen emerged from an open audition, held at the Pineapple Dance Centre in Covent Garden, one snowy January Saturday, though Anthony had worked with him before.

Once Anthony knew who the dancers were, he found it easier to work out possible scenarios, using their particular talents. He would discuss his ideas with Andrew, John Caird, and Wayne, they would say what they liked and what they didn't and Anthony would go away and think some more. While the overall storyline and characters were important, the choreography had to come first because the music dictates the mood of each section. 'At its most basic,' Wayne said, 'you can't have a slow lyrical dance to a fast, energetic piece of music.'

Anthony started work on the choreography by listening to the music over and over again on headphones, until he knew every note by heart, and pictures – not movements exactly – began to appear in his mind's eye. 'When I've listened enough,' Anthony said, 'it becomes very clear, and so when I get into the studio, all I have to do is make it happen! I don't like having things worked out in great detail before we start because that inhibits the creative process. I like throwing ideas to the dancers, setting them problems if you like, and seeing how they solve them. To me, that's what choreography is about.'

From the beginning, Anthony worked very closely with Wayne. 'He is so creative and has such a great eye for what makes good theatre that it would be stupid of me not to make full use of it. I think the mistake a lot of choreographers make with Wayne is to try and impose things on him which means that the work loses out on the considerable contribution he has to make.'

Obviously, having thought about the dance possibilities of 'Variations' himself, Wayne had lots of ideas to share with Anthony. 'I felt Variation 19–20 should be my solo because the music is very fast, very "up" which immediately suggests jumps, but there are quieter passages too, which have dramatic possibilities. I also felt that Variation 16, the Fugue, would be good for a big company tap number, because it is very noisy – lots of contrapuntal things going on – and very strange, but it does have a good steady beat all the way through it. I also felt that Linda Brewer and I should do a tap duet – we'd tapped together in Dash and it had gone down very well. A conversation between feet was what I had in mind, but there was nothing in the music to suggest that, so Andrew agreed to compose something specially for it.'

Although Anthony had some experience of tap, he would be the first to admit that it was too limited to choreograph the sort of routine Wayne had in mind. So Wayne asked around and eventually met Anne Emery, one of the stars of the children's television series 'Rentaghost' and a marvellous tap dancer, taught in the fifties by the legendary black American, Buddy Bradley. Wayne much admired her style which was 'into the ground, not up in the air, like the English!'

As for the set, it was agreed that it should be as simple as possible, relying mainly on lighting for the effects. With that in mind, award-winning lighting designer David Hersey was invited to design both the set and the lighting.

On 16 January Wayne gave his final performance in *Cats*, and flew off next day for a well-earned holiday in the Virgin Islands, though, as usual, he found it impossible to switch off altogether. While he was sitting on the beach or sailing round the islands in a yacht, he listened to 'Variations' through the headphones of his stereo cassette player.

He got back to London in early February. While he had been away, Robin Don had been approached to design the costumes and David Hersey had finished the designs for the set – basically a black box, with a W-shaped, light holding glass screen on to which slides would be projected, and three black metal gantries, with stairs and platforms, which would be moved around the stage.

Wayne was happy with the set, though he was worried because David wanted to put a false floor on the stage, cut in a W-shape at the front to reflect the shape of the screen which, Wayne felt, would give them even less space to dance in. 'They'd decided to have the band on stage in Marti's half, and they wanted to keep them there for ours. I didn't want that, because, first, I felt it was essential for our half to look completely different from Marti's, and second, the movement of the musicians would have been very distracting. It's okay when you have a singer who's more or less static, but not when you've got a lot of dancers leaping around the stage! So we agreed that they would be behind a black curtain during the second half.

'I had specified the surface we needed to dance on, a thin vinyl, and pointed out that if they were going to make grooves in the stage to take the wires that would pull Marti's gantry and the band trucks downstage, they'd have to make them the shallowest, narrowest grooves ever, or we wouldn't be able to dance on them.'

A few days after Wayne got back from the Virgin Islands, the Opera House rang him to ask if he would dance the Neapolitan Dance in *Swan Lake* the following Saturday, because it was to be Nureyev's first performance there for years. 'I said, "Of course I can't", but then, when I'd put the phone down, I thought, "Oh why not?" So I rang back and said I'd changed my mind! Next day, I was rehearsing. Of course, I hadn't danced at all for three weeks, and I had only five days to get back into shape. I did a crash course – went straight back into a full ballet class – and it was agony! My calf muscles were up in my kneecaps, and for the first few days, I couldn't walk downstairs! But then I was totally back into it. It's astonishing how quickly you lose it, and how quickly you get back into it again!'

Swan Lake went extremely well, though Wayne had been anxious beforehand about the reception he might get from the audience. 'I hadn't danced at the Opera House for over a year, and what's more I had really sent up classical ballet on "The Goodies" on ITV a few weeks earlier, so I thought they might throw rotten fruit at me! They didn't though – they applauded when I came on, which doesn't happen often, and I took three curtain calls at the end, which was lovely.'

Sunday was Wayne's last free day before rehearsals began. He slept late, and spent the afternoon quietly at home in his tiny, functional top floor flat in Covent Garden which he shares with his cat, Grace. 'She is half Abyssinian and very intelligent – she talks to me all the time! I got her nine years ago when I lived in Notting Hill Gate because I discovered dozens of mice living in my oven. I never used it, you see, but the pilot light was always on, so it was a nice, warm place for them to live! The day I brought Grace home, they all disappeared, never to be seen again. Just as well, if she'd seen those mice she would probably have run a mile! She really does have a charmed life. She once fell off the window-sill here which is four floors up, and landed in the street. The only injury she had was a cut in her mouth!'

WEEK ONE

When Wayne set off for the first rehearsal at The Place, home of the London Contemporary Dance Theatre, he was full of enthusiasm. 'It's always exciting starting work on a new piece because at this stage everything is possible. It's also stimulating working with a new choreographer and a new company. Then you find out just how good everybody really is! A lot of people audition well, but once you start rehearsing, you have to lay yourself on the line. Of course, I've worked with most of the dancers before, but even so, there is always the possibility that they'll surprise me, or maybe that I'll surprise myself!'

In Studio 8, the entire *Song and Dance* company assembled at eleven o'clock. Once John Caird had introduced the members of the company to each other David Hersey, the designer, spent the rest of the morning with them. Using a model of the set, he explained exactly how the gantries and the screen were going to work.

Once the meeting was over, Anthony sent the rest of the company off to buy tap shoes, and then began working with Wayne on his major solo, to Variations 19 and 20.

The basic idea Anthony began with was that Wayne had been rejected by the others, cut off from them physically by the screen which had just come down. 'To me, that suggests my character is in a world of his own, inside his own head, if you like. The fact that the music is very energetic, very "up", with the occasional slow, reflective passage, also suggests that if he lets himself go, he might just burst into tears, but he won't because he's tough, strong. To a large extent, the music dictates what the steps should be. The strong up-beats in the opening passage just cry out for jumps, and then it's a question of filling in the spaces with small steps.'

By the end of the session, they had set about half of the solo, and Wayne was very happy with the first day's work.

On Tuesday morning, the 'Variations' company assembled in Studio 8 once more, ready to start work. Although there were changing rooms downstairs, most of the dancers preferred to change in the studio. Street clothes were draped over chairs and the *barre*, and bags of dance gear lay scattered all over the floor. The dancers did not work in smart lycra leotards and tights, or soft velour tracksuits that the dance craze has made so fashionable, but wore instead torn T shirts, laddered woollen tights, nylon overtrousers, thick leg warmers, all for the sole purpose of keeping vital muscles warm and supple. What Wayne wore was no exception – it was quite an occasion when his leg warmers actually matched!

'Obviously, you do get very hot and sweaty when you're rehearsing, so you go through a lot of clothes in a week. I have someone who comes in Mondays, Wednesdays and Fridays to do the washing, tidy up generally – I'm so untidy and the flat is so small that it would be like a tip otherwise – and do the odd bit of shopping. I very rarely cook; the closest I get to it is having a piece of steak or chicken in the fridge which I watch going mouldy over the course of the week! I eat out most nights – I like Italian food, Chinese, Greek, and Indian sometimes, though not when I'm working because it's too heavy. I'm not a health food freak – far from it. I never eat eggs because I don't like them, and I'm not keen on dairy products either – but I really love McDonalds' hamburgers – and chocolate. I often have a bar of chocolate first thing in the morning to give me a burst of energy. I never bother with breakfast – some mornings I'll only have a glass of water! Chocolate apart, I don't like sweet things, which is just as well because I do have a weight problem. I put on weight very easily, and when you're small, even a few extra pounds show!'

Then the morning's rehearsal began. Since most of the dancers had never done any tap dancing before, and those who had, had only learnt the bare minimum, they were going to have tap lessons every day with Anne Emery. As they were all also going to be singing with Marti and Wayne at the end of the show, they were having daily singing lessons too, with Robert Purvis or Harry Rabinowitz, the show's musical director.

While Anthony worked with the others on the few sections that didn't involve Wayne, Wayne was at the nearby Euston Hall. He was working with Linda Brewer and Anne Emery, deciding on the steps they would use in their duet and learning them.

Wayne learnt tap when he was five, before he started ballet, but gave it up when he was nine. 'I started again about four years ago because I was doing a television show, and as I already had a few jazz pieces in my repertoire, I thought it would be a good idea to add the tap. So I had a few lessons and found the basic steps came back almost at once. But it's like everything else, if you want to be good at it, you've got to do it all the time.'

Since the music for the tap duet was to be written specially, Andrew Lloyd Webber came along to the first tap rehearsals to decide what kind of piece it should be.

'Even if it was going to be a conversation between feet, we still needed something to base it on, and Andrew suggested we used London Weekend Television's South Bank Show theme, starting by tapping it out a couple of times. Once we began work, I realised the talking feet idea wouldn't hold up for long and we'd have to turn it into a proper tap routine.

'We have to be very careful about the music, and getting Andrew to put in extra bits for us to dance to, because we're asking him to tamper with a very successful piece, which could actually suffer if it was treated in the wrong way. That's the trouble with working with living composers!'

On Tuesday evening, Wayne and Anthony worked on the solo again, putting together a series of dramatic jumps, spins, rolls and knee-slides, and ending with Wayne's celebrated multiple turns *à la seconde*. 'Although they come at the end of a long hard day, I find these evening sessions very productive, probably because when

Above and overleaf : Getting to grips with the tap duet – Linda Brewer, Anne Emery, Anthony, and Wayne, living up to the slogan on his T-shirt!

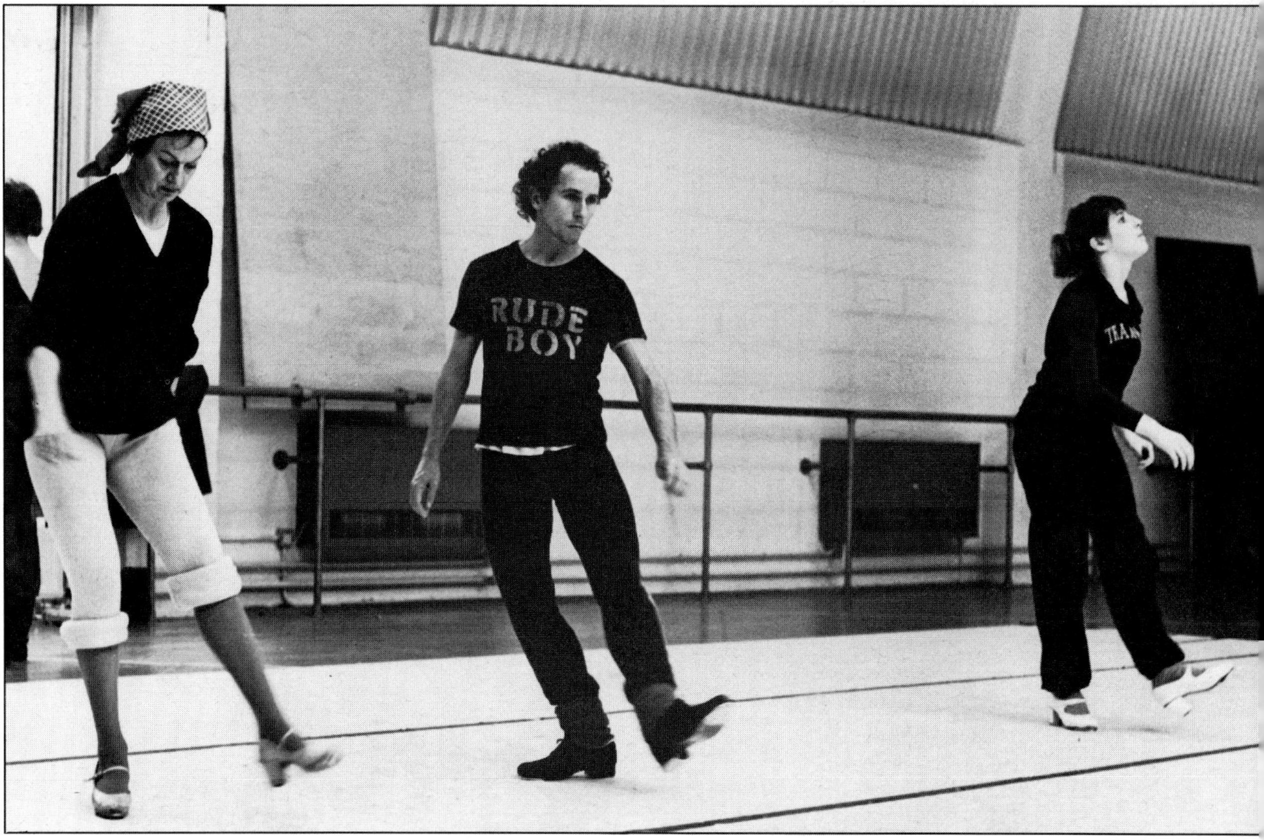
RUDE
BOY

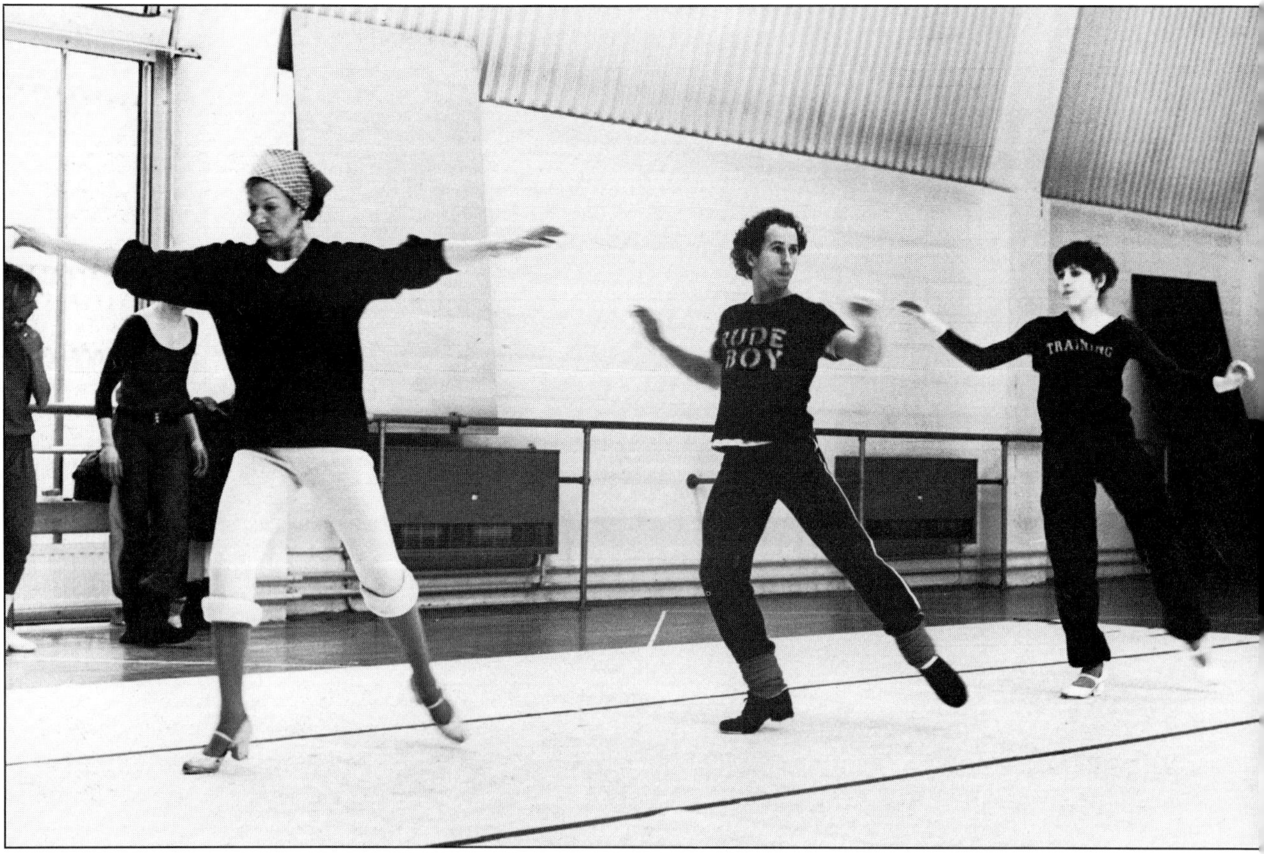
RUDE
BOY
TRAINING

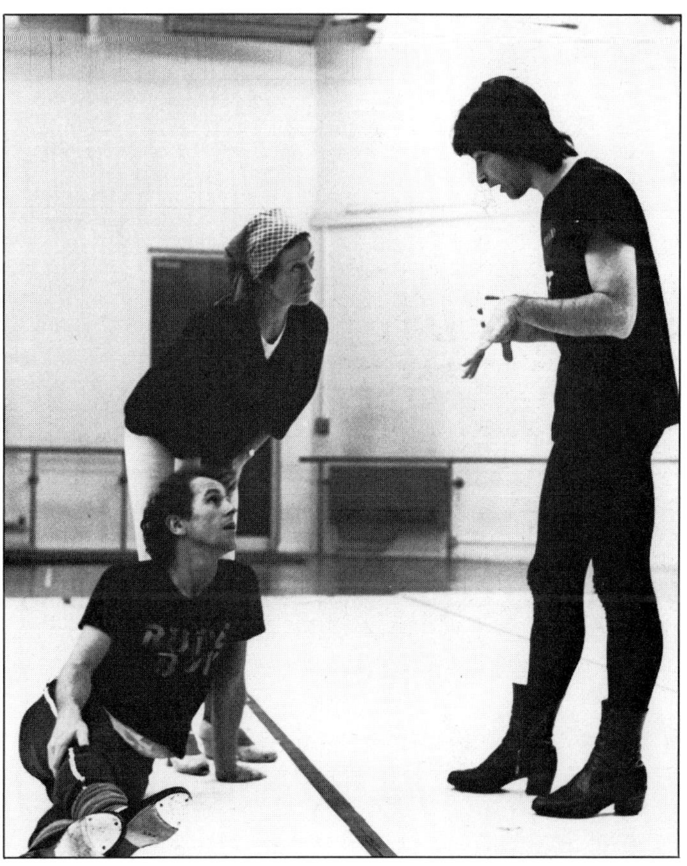

you're used to performing on stage at eight o'clock every night, the adrenalin starts going in the evening. The problem then is that though you're physically tired by ten o'clock, the adrenalin is still pumping round, and it takes hours to wind down before you're able to sleep. But then there really isn't anything to do in London at that time of night, except go to a restaurant, and when I'm rehearsing, I'm usually not very hungry. Thank God for Video! Most nights I go home and watch an old movie – that's what keeps me sane these days.'

Left : Robert Purvis going over the specially composed tap music with Andrew Lloyd Webber (centre) and Wayne

Wayne and Linda Brewer went through the tap again on Wednesday with Anne Emery at Euston Hall, while Anthony finished the lyrical duet with Paul Henry and Linda Gibbs, and started the jazz trio to Variation 9 with Jane, Sandy and Andy. A few weeks earlier, Andrew Lloyd Webber had done his own television show, and had asked Anthony to choreograph that particular Variation for Paul Henry and Finola Hughes, star of *Cats*. This meant Anthony had been able to try out some of his ideas, so he could set the trio very quickly.

On Wednesday evening, Wayne and Anthony went into the studio to put the finishing touches to the solo. But Wayne had been thinking about it and reached the conclusion that it wasn't really working. 'It seemed to me that we were throwing in pyrotechnics – jumps and spins – just for the sake of it, and they weren't actually saying anything. When I told Anthony, he laughed and said he'd reached the same conclusion but was waiting for me to say it!'

They took out one of the rolls, both the knee-slides which were already giving Wayne problems with his right thigh, and the multiple turns at the end, because they both felt they were throwing away one of their trump cards too early. So they rebuilt the

Opposite : Bringing the girls into the 7–8 Dance

solo, keeping the steps they liked and replacing those they didn't. By the time they finished, at ten, they both felt it was a great improvement.

'We'll leave it now, move on to other sections and come back to it later. Obviously, what comes before it and what comes after will affect it to some extent, so there's no point in polishing it yet because we may well find, once it's in context, that it doesn't quite work. Anyway, John Caird hasn't put in his two pennyworth yet, telling me what my motivation is for all this jumping about! No, seriously, that's very important. Even if I'm only smiling I have to know *why* I'm doing it!'

In the course of Thursday morning Robin Don came to watch the dancers at work, and get some inspiration for the costume designs. Wayne felt the costumes were going to be one of the hardest things in the whole production to get right. 'They've got to look "designed", not like dance gear we've just bought at the Pineapple Dance Centre, but they mustn't look theatrical and glittery. Quite what my costume will be like, I don't know, but for the end of the tap, I'll be wearing a jacket covered in tiny light bulbs, which will look sensational in the dark.'

On Thursday evening, Wayne and Anthony worked on the men's dance to Variations 7 and 8 which was instantly labelled the 7–8 Dance. 'This was the chance for the men to show off their strength, virility and sheer dancing ability, which male dancers in this country rarely get the opportunity to do.'

After the usual tap session at Euston Hall on Friday, Wayne joined Marti Webb at The Place for a photo session and brief interview with *The Sunday Telegraph* magazine. 'That's the last interview I'll do until after we open. Of course, it's very important to promote the show, but the work is what matters most and you have to cut out everything that distracts you from it.'

After the singing class and the company tap class, Anthony started work with Wayne and the other boys on the 7–8 Dance, but quickly realised that without the girls, it wouldn't build to the climax he hoped for. Besides, it would be asking too much of the boys to dance the whole piece at the same pace as the first section. So, he decided to include the girls.

Wayne went home on Friday night, well satisfied with the first week's work. 'It's been great fun so far. I always enjoy the early stages because you're not tired, you're still full of energy and enthusiasm and I also really like the exploratory nature of the work, feeling your way through a piece.

'It's also useful having John Caird around to talk to the dancers about their characters, which doesn't happen to dancers very often, and it's great to have help in forming your identity within the piece. But as John says, this piece is going to be so physically demanding that unless we really *want* to do it every night, we're not going to get through it!'

WEEK
TWO

Monday began for Wayne like almost every other day of his life, with class. If he has time, he goes to the Royal Ballet School in Hammersmith. If not, he goes to the Pineapple Dance Centre in Covent Garden, about a minute's walk from his flat. 'I always try and arrive about thirty seconds before the teacher walks in because then I'm forced to stay. If I got there ten minutes early and gave myself time to think about it, I'd never put myself through all that agony! And it is agony – a ballet class uses every muscle in your body so that at the end of an hour, you're exhausted. Once I get started, I concentrate totally on what I'm doing. It must never become automatic because the whole point is to correct your body, to get rid of bad habits that have crept in.'

Even getting to class in the morning is no mean achievement in itself because for Wayne, as for every other dancer, pain is a constant factor in his life. 'When you're working on a new piece, you wake up in the morning quite literally unable to move. Getting out of bed is a slow, painful business and as for walking to the bathroom, well . . .! When you're doing a new step, it twists your muscles in a way that they haven't been twisted before, and naturally, their reaction is to stiffen up on you, and hurt! What makes it worse is that early on in rehearsals you do a new movement, not once, but ten or fifteen times over. For instance, I'm having problems with my right thigh at the moment from all those slides along the floor in my solo. We've cut them now, but the damage was already done.'

Wayne spent the morning working with Linda Brewer and Anne Emery at the Euston Hall rehearsal room on the tap duet, and after a singing class at lunchtime, started working with Anthony and Paul Tomkinson on their acrobatic duet to Variation 15. The idea was that Paul would do an increasingly impressive series of gymnastic tricks while Wayne would pretend to follow suit, but end up doing one tame, ordinary forward roll instead. It took only twenty minutes to set the whole piece because they all knew what that section was about and the music, to a large extent, dictated how it should go.

That evening, Wayne again worked with Linda Brewer and Anne Emery on the tap duet. 'The ideas behind this section are beginning to emerge. My character gets involved with Linda's, but then gets so carried away with the tapping that he forgets all about her, and so she goes off with someone else. That happens in life a lot – people get so wrapped up in themselves and their careers that their relationships suffer.'

On Tuesday morning, Andrew Lloyd Webber arrived to compose the extra music Wayne and Linda needed to take them up and down the gantry steps in the tap duet. They gathered round the piano and, using the model of the gantry, counted the steps. Then Andrew sat down at the piano and fifteen minutes later had produced the extra bars they needed.

The rest of the day was spent working on the boys' section of the

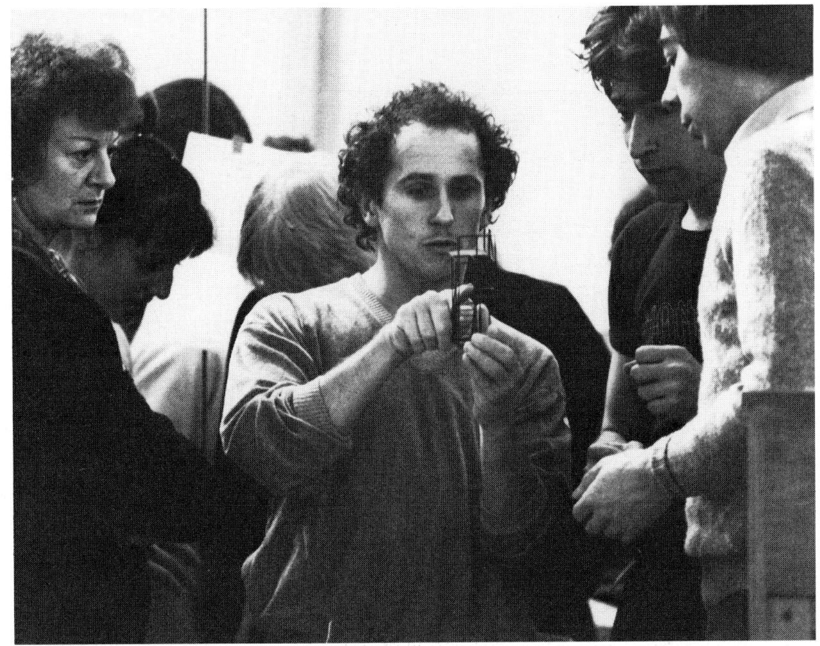

7–8 Dance, changing one of Wayne's jumps to a pull-back – 'With all the boys on stage, there really wasn't room for that jump, and it's not as though I'm not doing any in that section!' – and setting the acrobatic section at the end.

At six, Wayne had to leave to get ready for another performance of *Swan Lake* at Covent Garden.

On Wednesday, Wayne and Linda worked with Anne Emery at Euston Hall on the steps to take them up and down the gantries.

'We'll be eight feet up, remember, on a very small platform,' Wayne said to Anne. 'There'll be nothing to hold on to, so make it simple!'

Anne demonstrated a sequence of steps flat out, repeated it more slowly, and then broke it down into individual steps for Wayne and Linda to learn.

Wayne admitted that he was finding the tap hardest of all to master. 'I still haven't got it – nothing like – and once I leave the studio, it goes straight out of my head. I'll just have to keep going over it again and again until it's second nature. It's so fast that if you *do* stop and think about what comes next, you've had it! The problem with tap if you're ballet-trained is that you're trying to make your feet go the wrong way all the time. With ballet, you're pointing your toe, but with tap, it's all heel. It's all against the logic, too. Your weight is on one foot, and yet that's the foot you've got to move! But the main worry isn't physical, it's mental. I think of tap as *The Times* crossword for the feet. But like everything else, it's a matter of concentration and determination. If I make up my mind that I'll get it right, then I will.'

During the lunchtime singing class the show's musical director, Harry Rabinowitz, was trying to explain the technique of diaphragmatic breathing, and enlisted Wayne's help. Wayne

pulled up his jumper to expose his stomach, and demonstrated very graphically what Harry meant. 'For singing, you let your stomach and diaphragm out, lift your rib cage, and fill it with air, which feels really weird if you're a dancer because you are always thinking about your line. It goes against the grain to stick your stomach out as if you were pregnant and so you're taught to breathe the other way – in your back, keeping your stomach in and your rib cage down. Breathing correctly is vitally important for dancers because what makes you tired is *not* that your leg muscles aren't strong enough – it's the lack of oxygen in your blood, starving the muscles.'

After a run-through of the 7–8 Dance, Wayne started work with Linda Gibbs, Anthony and John Caird on their duet, where Wayne has replaced Paul Henry in Linda's affections. Since Paul was all straight-limbed and stretched, Wayne suggested that he should be more sinewy and serpentine.

He and Linda began experimenting with various movements, and then Wayne, standing behind her, took hold of her raised leg and moved it in a figure-of-eight, a movement everyone liked. By six o'clock, when everyone broke for supper, the bones of the duet had been set.

Rehearsals went on after supper, and Wayne and Linda Brewer ran through the tap duet for Anthony for the first time. They realised that it just wasn't working. It was too bitty, and Wayne felt the music was repeating the South Bank theme just too often. Anthony started working on the duet with them, putting the 'dance element' – jumps, turns and movement – on top of the tap steps Anne had devised.

On Thursday, Wayne and Linda Brewer started their day at The Place discussing with John Caird the ideas behind their first duet – the Crazy Dance to Variations 11 and 12. 'This section has to establish the nature of our relationship, which is basically crazy and knockabout, firmly in the minds of the audience *before* the tap.'

Later, they started working on the link between Paul Henry's duet with Linda Gibbs, and her duet with Wayne. Paul and Wayne had a quick, whispered conference about what they should do, then proceeded to show Anthony. While Paul was still standing with Linda, Wayne strutted on, fixed Paul with a look, and jerked his head dismissively, at which Paul burst into noisy tears, rubbing his fists into his eyes!

When everyone finally stopped laughing, they worked on the link in earnest. Then Wayne and Paul Tomkinson went over the acrobatic routine they had set the previous day. Wayne thought it would be fun if he could play a trick on Paul, competing by foul means, since he couldn't by fair! After some discussion, they decided that Wayne would encourage Paul to try a particularly difficult trick which he would then, apparently, fail to pull off and wind up flat on his back. Wayne would then laugh, give him the 'thumbs down', and run away.

Left, opposite and below: Wayne, Paul Henry and the other boys working out the acrobatic section of the 7–8 Dance

After the tea break, they started work on the link between the 7–8 Dance and the jazz trio, in which Wayne and Linda Gibbs were to dance together again briefly before she rejects him and rejoins the others. Wayne hadn't been happy about it all along. 'I didn't think that Linda rejecting me made sense in terms of the story. If she was meant to be doing it because I couldn't resist joining in with the boys in the 7–8 Dance, then why does she join in, too? It's not as though she's standing back, watching me show off. To me, it was just another dance starting for no real reason, and if we're not very careful, the piece is going to be too bitty, all broken up into twenty-three separate variations. Obviously, I'd like to dance more with Linda, but it just wasn't right there.'

...pposite and below: Feeling
...eir way ... Wayne and
...nda Gibbs working on the
...rly, exploratory stages of
...eir duet with Anthony and
...hn Caird

...verleaf: Wayne's
...enomenal jumping ability on
...ow in the boys' section of the
...–8 Dance

Anthony didn't want to cut the link altogether. Instead, they decided that Linda would rejoin the others, while Wayne moved among them, looking for her, trying to pull her out, but failing, which seemed to work very well.

At the end of the day, everyone sat around on the floor and relaxed amid piles of clothing, empty coffee cups and full ashtrays while Wayne regaled them with tales of his days at White Lodge, the Royal Ballet's junior boarding school in Richmond Park. 'When I went to sleep, I'd tuck my toes under the rail at the end of the bed to make my feet point! I'd wake up in the night with agonising cramp, and in the morning, my insteps were so painful that I could barely hobble into class!'

On Friday morning, Wayne felt so tired after the week of long rehearsals and his performance at Covent Garden, that he decided to sleep late, missing class for once, and felt much better for it.

The morning's work began with a run-through of everything they had set so far, from the Paul Henry–Linda Gibbs duet, to the Wayne and Linda Brewer tap routine. The other dancers had never seen the tap right through before and, deservedly, it got a round of applause.

Anne Sinclair, the costume supervisor, came along for the first time. It was her job to turn Robin Don's designs into costumes, and she was a little anxious that he had still not finished.

Later that morning, Robin arrived to show John Caird the designs for the four boys' costumes, and to talk to Wayne about what he would wear. Wayne had very clear ideas about the kind of outfit he wanted. 'I'd like a very up-to-date, well-cut pair of trousers, slightly pleated at the waist, but coming in at the ankles, like track-suit bottoms, so that they're soft and loose, but also formal. I don't want them too high-waisted – if I'm not careful, I look like a baby in a romper suit!'

John Caird suggested the outfit should be cream or white because this was the colour Marti would be wearing in the first half, and because it had the 'everyman' feel he wanted. Wayne wasn't keen on white because it makes him look very wide, and thought grey would be better.

After lunch, Wayne, Jane and Andrea started work on their trio. Since the music for Variations 13 and 14 (varied) involved two distinct themes, Anthony's idea was that Wayne should be involved with two different women at the same time, reflected in two very different styles of dance, classical ballet and jazz. The *motifs* he started with were squares for Andrea, and circles for Jane.

Wayne felt this section should be about him two-timing the girls. 'They don't know about each other, but as their individual sections of music get shorter and shorter, it suggests that I'm finding it more and more difficult to keep them apart. It's just like dating two girls at once – you have a series of near-misses, and then one night, they both show up at your place for dinner ...'

By the end of the day, they had set half the trio, and Wayne's only worry was that as it followed the tap, he might not have enough time to get out of his tap shoes into his jazz shoes. But Bob West, the company manager, remembering the shoe-changing problems Wayne had had on *Cats*, said he would make sure it was all sorted out very early on.

After the evening meal break, Wayne and Anthony started work on the opening. It was clear that the original idea, involving an intricate system of lighting effects in which the dancers appeared on stage as if by magic, was going to be too complicated, so they had to think again.

Wayne wanted a very cool beginning. 'The music is jolly and danceable but it isn't dynamic or big, so I wanted to echo that by starting small and building. What we came up with was a movement that built from the hips, to the feet, to the shoulders, then the head, finishing off with a double turn.'

Anthony suggested that Wayne started in the *Song and Dance* poster position – head thrown back, right arm pointing skyward – but Wayne felt it was too dramatic. They agreed, instead, that he would start crouching and slowly unwind. An hour later, they had set the opening up to the point where Wayne introduces the other dancers.

Looking back, Wayne felt on the whole that it had been a good week. 'It's coming together nicely, and we've had some very constructive sessions. I did get a bit edgy mid-week, but I knew that was because I was so tired. The thing that worries me, personally, most is the tap, but I know that'll be all right if I keep at it. I'm also worried about the overall concept of *Variations*. It's not a Glen Tetley ballet, it's a West End show, and the ideas must be strong and simple – they can't be too subtle. I feel the storyline is getting in the way at the moment, but I suspect all the character links may well disappear eventually, as my link with Linda Gibbs did yesterday. But it doesn't matter because we are using the characters to give us a skeleton to hang the flesh on, which is very valuable.'

On Sunday, Wayne had lunch with friends, and went to see the film *Reds*. 'When I'm working on something new, it's important to try and have a few hours' break from it to give my brain a chance to recharge. When I start work on a new show, I give it my total commitment, which means that during rehearsals, I really have no other life. I'm either working, thinking about work, or asleep!'

WEEK THREE

After a relaxing Sunday, Wayne was refreshed and ready to start work on Monday morning after class. He ran through the tap duet with Linda Brewer and then, with Andrea, Jane and Anthony, carried on setting the trio which they had begun on Friday afternoon.

After an hour, they had set it all, apart from the ending. 'Because it's a comedy number, it's got to have a strong ending, a punchline if you like. I hate putting endings on things until I've explored every possibility because the ending does set the seal on the whole number, and on what comes next.'

While Anthony and the rest of the company worked on their entrances after Wayne's solo, Wayne and Anne Emery went out to the staircase at the back of The Place to work on the steps he and Linda Brewer would do as they went up and down the gantries. After experimenting with a number of different steps, they decided that simplicity was the best policy and that a straightforward run up and down would be the most effective.

Back in Studio 8, Anthony was ready to start setting the company tap – Variation 16. During the first two weeks, while Wayne and Linda Brewer worked on their duet, the other seven dancers, four of whom had never tapped before, had learnt the techniques and the steps they would be using. Now, Anthony was going to put it all together in a routine.

Wayne sat on the floor, with Anthony, suggesting different arm movements to punctuate the crisp, machine-like quality Anthony was after. They worked on it nearly all afternoon, going over it again and again. For most dancers, it was by far the hardest routine to learn, because while classical ballet, contemporary and jazz have a lot in common, tap is unlike anything else.

Wayne felt that, at last, he was beginning to master the tap, and he wasn't really worried about it any more. 'Now my biggest worry is about pacing myself through the show because I'm never off-stage. But until I do the first run-through, I won't know just how hard it's going to be.'

Before the evening meal break, Wayne and Anthony talked about Variation 17, the section between his trio with Andrea and Jane, and his solo, and agreed, in general terms, what it would say.

'Anthony had deliberately left it blank so that we could use it to tie up any loose ends or fill in any gaps. Since it comes just before my solo, where the screen comes down and cuts me off from the others, we felt there had to be a clearly stated reason for my being left on my own. So, what we've decided is that I'll dance briefly with each of the four girls, in their own styles – a reprise of what we'd done together earlier – then they'll each reject me and go off with their partners. It's like splitting up with your girlfriend – you try ringing round all your old girlfriends to see if you couldn't give it one more try, and find they don't want to know!'

On Tuesday therefore, when Anthony started work with the company on Variation 17, it took very little time to set. Then they moved on to the second half of the company tap, and worked out Wayne's entrance, Linda Brewer's, and the hornpipe section. Finally, they ran through the whole of the tap, at full speed, and apart from the odd collision, and the wrong arm going up here and there, it went very well.

After the tea break, Wayne, Andrea and Jane worked with Anthony on their trio, trying to come up with an ending. Anthony suggested that Wayne lift Andrea above his head in a *présage*, while Jane ran her hands up and down his thighs. Wayne thought it would look even more effective if he waggled his hips at the same time. 'My idea was that I'd be ballet from the waist up and jazz from the waist down, but waggling my hips nearly killed me! It's years since I lifted anybody, though that wouldn't be a problem by itself because the girls are so light. But doing what I'm doing is pulling every muscle I have from the wrists down!'

Anthony suggested that as Wayne brought Andrea down, she went into a low Fish Dive, while Jane wrapped one leg round Wayne's neck. It was physically possible – just!

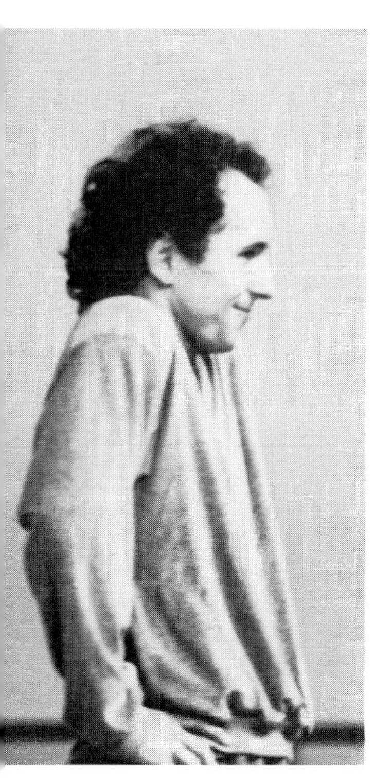

Right and overleaf: Wayne's trio with Andrea and Jane underwent more major changes during the course of rehearsals than any other section

'The thing is,' Wayne said, from somewhere inside a knot of limbs, 'how do we get out of this?'

It soon became clear that the only way was for them all to sink to the floor, still entwined, and untangle themselves as best they could.

'Maybe we ought to have the lights going down here,' Wayne said, 'so we can sort ourselves out in the dark!'

Wayne, Linda Brewer and Anthony then started work on the Crazy Dance, their first duet. Anthony had come up with some frenetic, rag-doll-on-speed type steps for them to do individually, but they needed steps they could do together. Wayne tried out a silly walk or two, one of which involved holding onto each other's ankles as they went along, which led to much falling over and giggling! But, as always, Wayne was quickly back to the matter in hand, concentrating on getting it right.

At the end of the session, though, he didn't feel that much progress had been made. 'In many ways, funny dances are the hardest of all to get right. It isn't enough just to throw yourself about – in fact, it's almost more important for a dance like this to be "clean", and perfectly timed than it is for a slow lyrical dance.'

When Wayne is rehearsing a new show, he finds it very difficult to fit in everything else. His time is at such a premium that he often has to combine two things at once, and during the evening meal break he had arranged to talk to the researcher from the Parkinson programme on which he had agreed to appear the following night, while he was having his hair cut at Trevor Sorbie in Covent Garden. 'I'm only doing it to plug the show, and my new record, *Man to Man*. It's a single, though it's packaged like an LP which has already created problems. Tony Blackburn played it on his radio show at the wrong speed!'

On Wednesday morning, after class, Wayne headed for one of his favourite shops, Ebony, in South Molton Street, to buy something new for his television appearance that night. Though he tends to wear old jeans, favourite hand-knitted sweaters and casual coats when he's working, he does like to splash out occasionally on very stylish, expensive clothes. This time, he bought a leather top, half French navy, half white.

Back at The Place, the company ran through the whole of the tap section for John Caird who had been away with the Royal Shakespeare Company for a few days, and hadn't seen it before. He was delighted.

After Anthony had set Variation 5 (varied) – the section after Wayne's solo, which is a reprise, musically and choreographically of Linda Gibbs's and Paul Henry's lyrical duet and so didn't take long to work out – he moved on to the last-but-one section, Variation 22. In this the couples split up and become individuals again.

They had been working for about an hour when someone Wayne didn't know came in to watch the rehearsal. It made him so angry that he stopped work, got changed, picked up his bag and left for the day. 'I don't want to be seen rehearsing by people who don't know me or my work. It embarrasses me when I'm still fumbling in the dark, and if I'm inhibited by the presence of strangers, I'm not going to do my best work. I'm certainly not going to risk experimenting.'

That evening, he recorded the Parkinson show, with fellow guests Jenny Agutter and Lord Kilbracken. He was interviewed last, and talked about the pain dancers live with, about *Cats*, and his own cat, Grace, and briefly about *Song and Dance*, which was the reason he had been asked to appear. 'Anthony van Laast, the choreographer, has done a marvellous job,' he told Michael Parkinson, 'but thanks to you, I've got two hours off rehearsals tonight!'

On Thursday morning, Anthony had decided that what was needed between the end of the tap and the start of Wayne's trio with Andrea and Jane was a silent variation with Linda Brewer and Sandy Strallen.

While Anthony was working with Linda and Sandy, Wayne and Anne Emery disappeared into the gents changing room, the only empty room they could find, to go over the steps for his tap solo at the end of the company tap, and for his exit. Anne pom-pommed the music, while Wayne experimented with different combinations of steps until he hit on one that he liked. The final hour of the session was spent setting the first half of the finale, with all the dancers in a wedge-shaped formation moving slowly downstage.

As Wayne was getting changed to go to the Royal Opera House where he was dancing in *Swan Lake* again, the lyrics of the song which he and the company would be singing with Marti at the very end of the show arrived, along with Wayne's harmony. Robert Purvis played it through for him on the piano, while Wayne la-la'd along.

Although Wayne had spent the day learning new steps and listening to new rhythms, he had no difficulty in switching off and preparing himself for the Neapolitan Dance in *Swan Lake*. 'Psychologically, there is no difference as far as I'm concerned between doing a tap routine on the stage of the Palace Theatre, and dancing in *Swan Lake* at Covent Garden. It's all dance, and though people are inclined to treat ballet as a sacred art, it *is* supposed to be entertainment after all!'

The next morning, the stage hands at the Palace Theatre had finished laying the false floor, so Wayne went along to have a look. 'The hole I was going to hide in after the acrobatics with Paul Tomkinson is much too wide for me to get completely out of sight, so I think now, I'll probably go under the stage, change into my tap shoes there and come up the other side for the tap.'

When Wayne arrived at The Place at lunch time, he learned that Robin Don had been taken into hospital with a suspected perforated ulcer. Most of the designs were finished, though, and

Anne Sinclair was taking over the finishing touches.

The company spent most of the afternoon working on the second half of the finale, an energetic all-running, all-jumping affair. 'The music seems a bit ploddy for a finale,' Wayne said, 'Couldn't we get them to speed it up a bit? It is only a matter of *tempo*. Mind you, if I know anything about theatre musicians, it'll be different every night anyway!'

During the tea break, everyone sat round on the floor, while Anthony and Wayne worked out the other dancers' positions on the gantries during the opening, using the model of the set and blobs of Blu-tak to represent the dancers.

'This is Wayne,' Anthony said, putting down the first blob on the model stage. Wayne looked at the blob, looked at Anthony, then picked up the blob, stretched it to twice its original height, and amid hoots of laughter, put it firmly back again!

On Saturday morning at The Place, the company did the first-ever run-through of *Variations* before a small audience made up of Andrew Lloyd Webber, Cameron Mackintosh and their respective staffs, who greeted it with enthusiastic applause. Wayne was quite happy with the way it had gone – or at least, he thought he was. 'I was still trying to remember all the steps, and it was very very hard, physically, just getting through it. The first complete run-through is always a shock to the system, and I was exhausted afterwards – my rib cage ached, and my breathing didn't get back to normal for about two hours!'

After the run-through the details of Wayne's costume still had to be discussed, so he had a late lunch with Anne Sinclair and Gordon Hutchings, who has made stage clothes for him for years. 'The trousers will be made of silver-grey leather, which looks great though we have to see whether or not I can dance in them! If I can't, I can always add them to my own wardrobe!'

It had been a tiring week for Wayne but, overall, he thought they had made good progress. 'I felt it was very important to get it finished this week, even if some bits were only sketched in because I need three weeks to work on my performance, and we have to be able to look at the overall shape and see if it works. The worst productions are those where they don't have time to change anything – they set the last step, and they're on!

'I think we have a good basis now for a forty-five minute dance piece. It isn't *War and Peace*, but there's enough of a story for it to make sense to the audience when we change from something lively to something slow and lyrical. We still haven't decided on what happens at the end – whether I'm still alone or whether I find fresh hope with someone new.'

WEEK FOUR

The fourth week of rehearsals got off to a bad start. The *Variations* company had been moved from Studio 8 at The Place into a new church hall in Chiswick which looked like a red-brick silo. Not only that, the room was freezing cold, had no mirrored walls or *barres* to warm up on, and the floor was slippery and too hard to risk jumping on. 'We can't work in conditions like this,' Wayne said. 'We could easily damage ourselves.'

While Anthony went to talk to Bob West, the company manager, about finding an alternative rehearsal room, Sue Hywel took the company through a strenuous ballet class to try and get cold muscles warmed up. Although everyone was sweating at the end of it, instead of peeling off layers of clothing as usual, they put more on!

It was decided that they would work only on sections that didn't involve jumping or lifting. They started with the tap, learning the changes that Anthony had made after Saturday's run-through, including the new ending. This involved Linda Brewer coming back on with a towel round her neck, and gesturing to indicate that everyone else had gone, and Wayne simply taking the towel from her with a curt nod, and walking off, still wrapped up in himself and his tapping.

Anthony had also decided after Saturday's run-through, with Andrew Lloyd Webber's backing, to extend the 7–8 Dance, and he began working with the girls on their new section.

Once it had been set, they ran through it a couple of times, just 'marking' the jumps for safety's sake. Wayne spent the rest of the afternoon working with Anthony and John Caird on the links between variations, in which he is instrumental in bringing couples together.

When Bob West arrived about 6.30, he still hadn't been able to arrange an alternative rehearsal room for the rest of the week. 'I'm going to do class at the Royal Ballet School tomorrow morning,' Wayne said, 'and if you want me to, I'll come in here afterwards and "mark" it (walk through it) in plimsolls, but I'm not dancing here – it's too dangerous.' When Bob pointed out that they had rehearsed *Cats* there for weeks, Wayne went on, '*Cats* wasn't an all-dancing show like this is, and the choreography wasn't as difficult or as good. It was mainly hips and very few jumps, but the floor is so hard that we didn't even do those few jumps here. But even so, Judi Dench snapped her Achilles tendon, which put her in hospital and out of the show!'

Anthony suggested that they settle for the large rehearsal room at the new Pineapple West Dance Centre off Baker Street, even though they would have to move out every lunchtime because it was already booked. While Bob went away to try and arrange it, everyone drifted off home. Wayne's chauffeur-driven Rolls Bentley was waiting outside to take him back to Covent Garden. 'It's my one real luxury – it's so comfortable! – and I have to have someone to drive it because I've never learnt how! But it doesn't come out of the garage very often. In town, it's easier to take taxis.'

On Tuesday, the company assembled in Studio I at Pineapple West, a huge barn of a room, with a high vaulted ceiling, but it was warm, had mirrors all along one wall and *barres* along the other three. At lunchtime, Wayne ran through his solo for the first time in several days, and both he and Anthony were pleased with the way it was coming together.

After the first, flat-out run-through of the extended 7–8 Dance, everybody collapsed, drenched in sweat, except Wayne who put on his tap shoes and went to work in one corner with Anne Emery on his entrance half way through the company tap.

Ten minutes later, he and Linda Brewer ran through the tap duet, but the acoustics in the studio were so echoey that they couldn't hear the piano clearly, and Robert couldn't differentiate taps from echoes of taps. The *tempo* went haywire, and he started playing faster and faster, until finally Wayne had to clap his hands to stop him!

In the meantime, Anthony had decided that the extended 7–8 Dance didn't work after all. The music had been very carefully structured by Andrew, he felt, and putting in an extra section would have ruined it. After the others had left for a singing call at six, Wayne, Anthony and John Caird went upstairs to one of the smaller studios to work on the end of his solo.

'Originally, I wanted silhouettes of the couples to come up on the screen after I've been cut off from them, so that I can see them but can't be involved with them, almost as though the images were really only in my mind. But that's not possible technically, so we'll have to think again.'

Before he left that evening, Wayne ran through his harmony for the finale song with Robert at the piano, and recorded it on his cassette recorder, so that he could play it over and over to himself at home – the only way he could learn it.

Making use of a few spare minutes, Wayne and Linda Brewer polish the tap duet in a small studio upstairs at Pineapple West

At seven, he had a costume fitting with Gordon Hutchings in Covent Garden. Gordon had made up the trousers in cheap black leather, just to see whether Wayne would be able to dance in them. Wayne slipped them on. They were too loose almost everywhere, so Gordon got to work with tailors' chalk and pins.

'They can't be too tight,' Wayne said, 'or I won't be able to lift my legs, and I think they'll have to be lined so that they'll slide easily up my thigh.'

Gordon had made up a rough, calico version of the top, and was having problems with the fit on the shoulders. 'The left one is higher than the right,' Wayne said, matter-of-fact.

The day still wasn't over for Wayne, and he left at half past seven for a meeting with his partner and *de facto* manager, George Lawson, to talk about the next Dash tour of Britain. 'We've decided that I should give an award to pay for a youngster to study dance – ballet, contemporary, jazz or tap – for a year. We'll hold auditions in every town we visit on the Dash tour, and choose one boy or girl from each to come to London for a final audition. It seems to me it's fairly easy for ten- or twelve-year-olds to get scholarships to recognised ballet schools, but fourteen- or fifteen-year-olds who've just decided they want to dance, don't stand a chance. So that's who the award will be for. George suggests we call it "The Sleep Late Developer Award", but we'll see!'

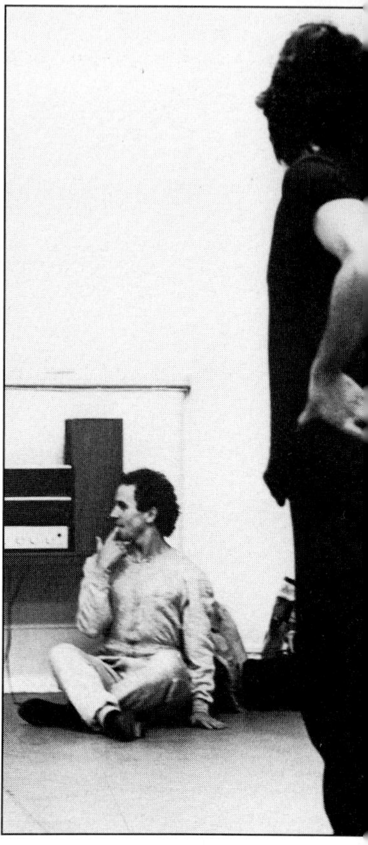

Decisions needed to be made about other aspects of the show and on Wednesday Jill and Naomi from GB Wigs came to watch the company at work. They would be doing the make-up, and cutting and colouring the dancers' hair where necessary, and they wanted to get an idea of character and of how much slog and sweat would go into each performance, so they could design hairstyles rigid enough to withstand it.

Then Anne Sinclair arrived with a pair of grey tap shoes for Wayne, made by Anello and Davide, to his own special last. He tried them on, but they dug into his heel, so he asked Anne to take them back and get them cut down a little.

Tap shoes created a problem on Thursday, too, when Wayne and Linda Brewer ran through the tap duet upstairs in Studio 5. 'I have Capezio taps on my shoes, but Linda has rattle taps on hers which are loose, so they rattle *after* she's tapped, and I can't hear whether she's just starting a beat or has just finished one, so I've suggested she gets them changed.'

Downstairs, after a run-through of the company tap, Wayne, Andrea and Jane started work on the trio, and Wayne had a bright idea. 'It suddenly dawned on me. It's not that the girls don't know about each other. They *do*, but they're both out to get me for themselves, so I'm being torn between them. The original two-timing idea was a good one, but it needed time to establish and this Variation just isn't long enough. The other problem was that it was quite a funny idea, but we've just had the tap, Andrea and Paul's duet and the Crazy Dance, which are also quite funny, so there was a danger of it becoming relentless fun. It's still a good basic idea, though, which I'll save and use in Dash!'

When the rest of the company went off for a singing call, Wayne stayed behind to run through his solo. He danced it flat out, but wasn't happy because he felt there wouldn't be enough space on the stage to do it justice. Anthony suggested that if he cut back underneath himself during the first series of jumps, instead of travelling forward, there wouldn't be a problem.

Wayne tried it again, but felt it was no better. 'Do a light show here, boys,' he said, 'I'm sick of dancing where there isn't enough space,' and walked away in disgust.

He was very angry that what he felt was a really good piece of dance was suffering from lack of space because of the W-shaped cut-out at the front of the stage. 'What we decided eventually was to speed up the music a little, make it a beat faster so that I didn't have as far to travel between notes, and rework the choreography slightly. Afterwards, Anthony, John Caird and I went and had a nice dinner at L'Escargot, enjoyed ourselves, and forgot all about it!'

Much of Friday morning was taken up by a film crew from Thames Television filming Wayne and Linda Brewer. Instead of the usual assortment of torn T shirts, tracksuit bottoms, and nylon dungarees, Linda was wearing a neat, black 'ra-ra' dress, and for once even Wayne's leg-warmers matched! Once filming was finished, the company spent the afternoon working on the link between Variation 22 and the finale, Variation 23.

During the tea break, Anne Sinclair arrived once more with Wayne's grey tap shoes, this time cut down at the heel as requested. 'They've also cut away half an inch all round,' Wayne said, trying them on, 'so now I can't get them to stay on my feet! It's a waste of a perfectly good pair of shoes.'

They were still rehearsing on Saturday afternoon, when they were back at The Place for the day. Wayne, Linda Brewer, Anthony and Sue Hywel worked on the Crazy Dance, about which Wayne had reservations. 'I found it very hard to get into this Variation because the music doesn't say anything to me. The other problem was to do with character – the idea for this dance is two crazy people who fancy each other, and wind up knocking each other around. But my character hasn't been crazy up to that point, so there seems no reason for me suddenly to become crazy. I think Linda should start off dancing on her own, I'm attracted to her, go over to try and calm her down, and get thrown on the floor for my pains. Finally, I realise the only way to pacify her is to use the same force on her as she uses on me.'

Although Wayne was happier about the Crazy Dance by the end of the session, the week as a whole hadn't been very satisfactory from his point of view. 'We should *never* have been moved out of The Place, because it takes you three or four days to settle down in somewhere new. On top of that, I was worried about the storyline. I was afraid we would wind up with half a message, which would be pretentious because it suggests that it's deeper than it really is.

'And basically, I didn't feel that the choreography was being challenged enough and that enough questions were being asked, which is why I asked them myself. I wasn't happy with the piece as it stood. It was on the right lines, but it wasn't *there* yet, and I feel a lot of things changed as a result.'

WEEK
FIVE

On Monday, 15 March, the company moved into the Palace Theatre. For many of them, it was their first time on a West End stage, and therefore very exciting, but, for an old hand like Wayne, it was just another step in the process of putting on a production.

'As long as the piece is ready, then the sooner you get into the theatre, the better. It's good to get away from mirrors, and find out whether the piece stands up without them, and you need as long as possible to get used to the feel of the stage, because it's quite different. For a start, the stage is raked (sloped towards the front), so you have to adjust your balance, and you also have to get used to dancing in the space you actually have. In the studio, we had the stage marked out with tape, but it didn't matter if you went over the edge. Do that on the stage, though, and you could break a leg!'

When the company arrived, they were allocated dressing-rooms – Wayne on the first floor with Marti, the other dancers upstairs. Then those who needed it, had their hair cut, permed and tinted.

Down on the stage, chaos reigned supreme. People were hammering, banging, drilling, shouting to – and at – each other. Wayne found a small space, and tried out a few steps. 'It's not bad at all, better than I thought it would be. In *Cats* the floor was virtually undanceable for the first two weeks, so this time, I've made sure that I was in on all the decisions about things like this. It's the only way to work!'

After a meeting in the red plush and gilt stalls bar, at which Anthony, John Caird, and David Hersey explained what would be happening during the next two weeks, the company assembled on stage, and began climbing over the gantries which they were seeing for the first time.

They finally started work, running through the opening, and trying out the positions which they had worked out ten days earlier. They went through the first few Variations, pointing up the links, adjusting positions, getting used to moving the gantries around the stage.

Anne Sinclair came with yet another pair of tap shoes for Wayne, but they still didn't fit. In exasperation, Wayne finally suggested that he should use his own pair of white tap shoes which could be dyed.

After the evening meal break, the four boys put on their costumes for the first time to show Anthony and John Caird. The only one they weren't happy with was Sandy's – too theatrical, they felt – but Anthony wanted time to think about how it should be changed.

At half past nine, the company did the first run-through on stage, stopping once or twice, and marking some sections. All in all, Wayne was pleased with the way it had gone. 'Everything we thought might not work, worked very well, and we'll only have to make a few slight changes to the choreography because of a lack of space.'

Below : Yet another pair of tap shoes that isn't right

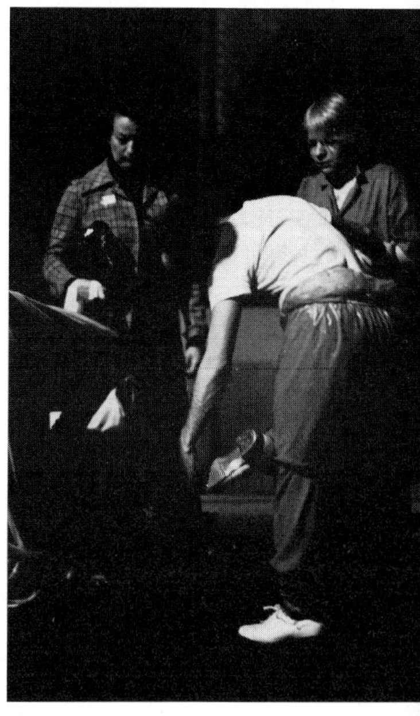

Opposite and overleaf : First day on stage at the Palace Theatre

On Tuesday Gordon Hutchings arrived with Wayne's costume for the first proper fitting. Wayne found he could move easily enough in the grey leather trousers, though he felt they were too baggy and too long, but he wasn't at all happy about the top. It made him look top-heavy he felt, and he didn't like the way it gaped open in the front. Gordon snipped off the pleats, and suggested pulling it tight with a crutch strap to stop it gaping, but it still wasn't right, so Anne suggested making it in lycra instead. She then showed Wayne the very expensive, quilted, embroidered bomber jacket she'd got on approval for the tap duet. Wayne didn't like it. 'I'd look like a dancing duvet in that!' he said. 'All I want is a *plain*, red satin baseball jacket.'

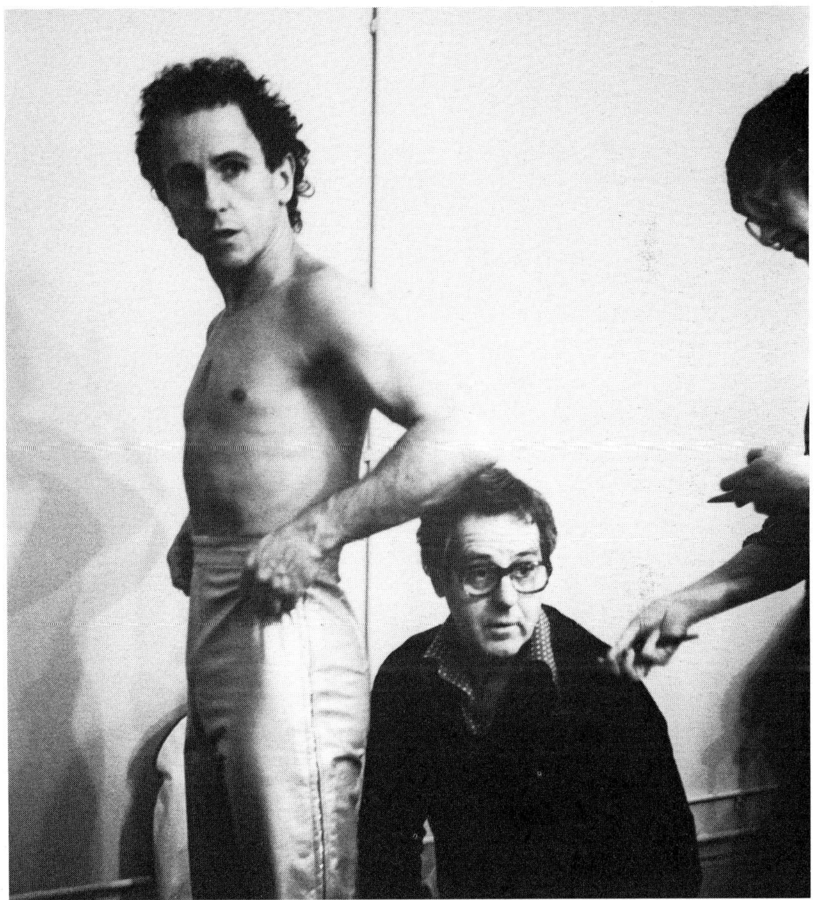

Robin had brought in strings of ring LEDs (light emitting diodes) in red and green which would be used on the jacket of lights, for Wayne's approval.

At two o'clock, the company started work on the second half of *Variations*, but Wayne found it hard to get going because he was tired and had been having difficulty sleeping. 'I'm counting all day, and my brain just won't switch off when I go to bed at night. Last night, for example, I also had pains in my arms and chest, and I was convinced that a heart attack was imminent! But I expect it was only muscular, from hauling myself up the gantries yesterday!'

He was also in a silly mood, and, in the gaps between bursts of activity, entertained the others with chunks from Peter Cook and Dudley Moore's rather rude 'Derek and Clive' albums, and his famous Bette Midler imitation.

Wayne giving Sue Hywel some stick

Before the run-through that evening, Wayne's main worry was whether he would have enough stamina to get through it. 'I haven't done it flat-out yet – last night, I was still marking parts of it – so I don't know if I'll be able to. But then, I don't think it'll work unless I *do*. Tonight, I'll give it all I've got, and see.'

Wayne danced flat-out all the way through. 'Stamina problem?' he said afterwards. 'What stamina problem?'

On Wednesday, Wayne, Jane and Andrea worked on their trio with Anthony. They were all happy with the choreography, but no one was sure how it fitted into the storyline. After all, both girls had already paired up with their final partners, so why would they both be after Wayne?

Wayne and the others talked about it, and came up with a better idea. 'The two girls have seen the rotten way I treat Linda Brewer after the tap, so they decide to teach me a lesson by doing the same sort of thing to me – playing with me, leading me on, then, at the end, pushing me away and going off with their own partners. I think that's much better because relationships are like that sometimes.'

Since the ideas behind the trio had changed, the choreography had to be altered slightly, too. It didn't need to be so starkly formal at the beginning, and the ending was different, with the girls spinning Wayne round, and pushing him down.

Since they had been discussing the storyline, Wayne admitted that he wasn't at all happy about his role in the first half. 'It doesn't make sense. I seem to spend the first part bringing people together, and at the same time, getting involved myself. So what am I meant to be? A master-of-ceremonies, outside the action, or one of the group, having relationships of my own?' After some discussion with Anthony and John Caird, it was agreed to change the links so that Wayne was no longer bringing people together.

While Wayne and David Hersey were discussing how he was going to get up to the top of Andrea's gantry during the opening section, and settling on a trapeze, there was a potential disaster on stage.

Linda Gibbs injured her left foot and couldn't stand on it. Obviously, with the opening performance just ten days away, everyone was extremely anxious and she was whisked off to hospital for an X-ray. There were no bones broken, so she made an appointment to see her own osteopath that night.

After the dinner break, the rest of the company worked with Marti on the song, and then set the rock 'n' roll finale which, with everyone contributing ideas, took less than an hour.

Once they had finished, Wayne changed into his costume for a photo session with Zoë Dominic for the slides which were to be projected onto the screen at the end of his solo. They were action shots, so he danced the solo for real, but the stress of all those jumps was too much for the leather trousers and they split right across one cheek!

'What a drag! At least if they'd split down a seam, Gordon could have mended them and I could have had them to wear off-stage! Now, he's going to make the trousers in the same colour lycra as the top, but at least the audience will see the leather ones every night, up there on the screen!'

The next day, to everyone's relief, Linda Gibbs's foot was all right and she was able to dance. But Wayne now had a medical, or rather a dental, problem. One of his wisdom teeth was giving him a lot of pain. 'The only answer is to have it out, but I really don't know when, because I don't want to miss any performances.'

pening positions for the inale – Variations 22 and 23

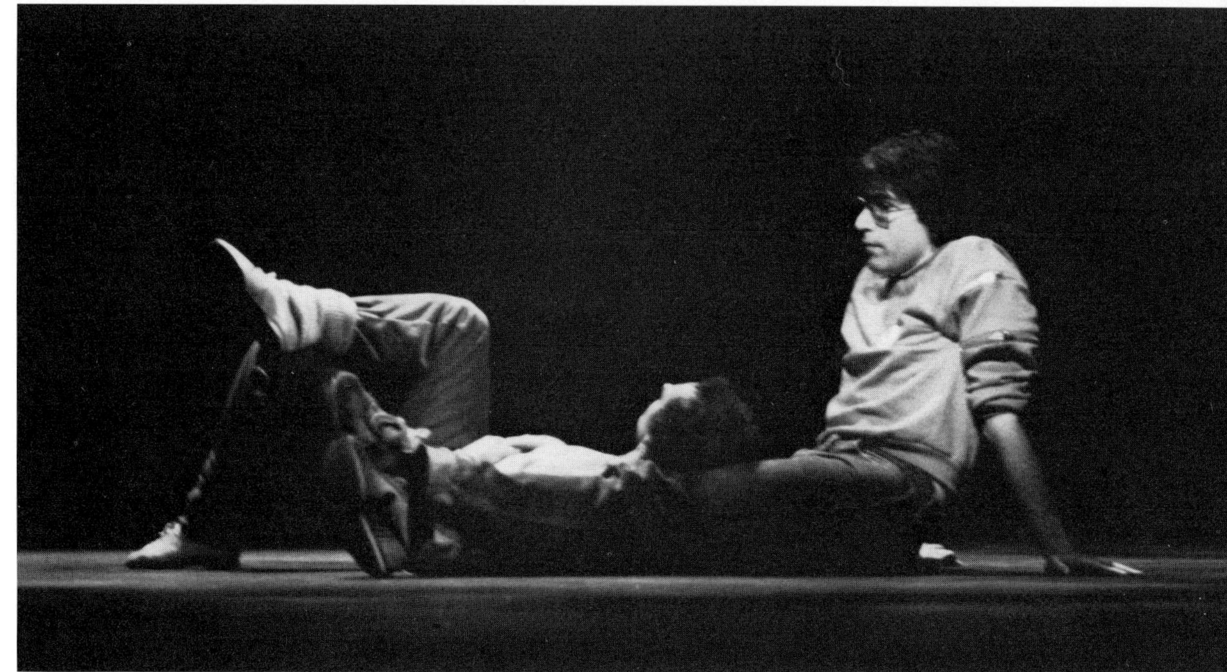

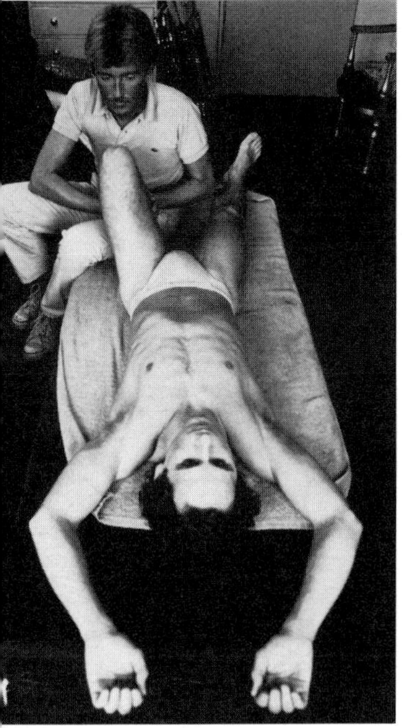

bove : A much-needed
ssage in the dressing-room

ight : Zoë Dominic takes the
ficial production stills of Jane
d the other dancers, but
ayne's new costume isn't
ady, so he fills the time as
st he can

That afternoon saw the first lighting call – a slow, tedious process for the dancers, with long periods of inactivity, while David Hersey worked on the lighting effects. So they sat around on the gantries, chatting, or swinging on the bars. Suddenly, the gantry on which Andrea and Paul Tomkinson were sitting started to topple over. Paul tried to stop it, but couldn't, and they both somehow managed to jump clear, as it crashed onto the stage. Astonishingly, neither of them was hurt.

During the course of the afternoon, George Lawson, Wayne's partner, arrived with a small fridge and a sofa for Wayne's dressing-room. 'I've been in grottier dressing-rooms and also in more comfortable ones. They've painted it for me, and screened off the end to give me somewhere to get made up, and they're going to put in a full-length mirror, and a short *barre*, so I can warm up, but I've had to bring in my own furniture!'

During the evening meal break, Wayne had asked his masseur to come to the theatre and give him a much-needed massage. 'I get him to pull all my joints out, starting with my ankles, working up my legs, to my spine, and neck, to elongate my body again. If I'm standing all day and especially if I'm doing lots of jumping, my joints do get compressed. If I can, I have a sauna at the same time. After you've been dancing, your feet and ankles do feel very pudgy and leaping into the cold plunge pool takes the swelling down.'

Another lighting call took up most of Friday, but Wayne made good use of the time, practising tap steps either alone or with Linda Brewer. After much thought, he and Anthony decided that tapping up and down the gantries didn't work. 'It was dangerous doing it in tap shoes because metal on metal is very slippery, but more important, the taps were just not making the right noise because the steps and platforms were made from metal mesh and the sound was just going right through. All in all it seemed best to lose it.'

At five o'clock, the others went off to put on their costumes and make-up for the first time, for a photo session with Zoë Dominic. Wayne's new trousers weren't ready, but he decided to try out his make-up anyway. It was fairly straightforward – pancake, shader to hollow his cheeks, powder, shiny blue eye-liner all round his eyes, blue mascara, and lip pencil just to define his lips.

'It's so difficult when you don't have lips *or* eyes,' Wayne said, gazing dispassionately at his reflection.

On Saturday, Wayne, Linda Brewer, Anne Emery and Anthony worked on the new section of the tap duet which was replacing the tapping on top of the gantries. 'We had no room to move up there, so the steps were designed to be done on the spot. Now we're down on the stage, there's no reason why we shouldn't move around, so we need different steps. Rather than lose the gantries altogether, we thought it would be fun if Linda heads for the stairs, which fits in with her zany, reckless personality, and I have to pull her back!'

In contrast with the previous week, Wayne felt that this had generally been a good week. 'I am a bit worried about the lighting. Some of it is very low-key and we really are having a problem seeing the front of the stage, but they say they'll sort that out next week.

'I've been thinking about my character a lot, too. Cutting the links where I was pairing people off has helped, and I've decided that I'll base my role on my relationship with Linda Brewer. When it doesn't work out with the other girls, it doesn't really matter, but when I lose Linda, I really regret it, and wish we could get together again. So when I'm all alone and sad at the start of the solo, it's because I've lost her. And as I dance more with Linda than with anyone else, the audience can see this was a relationship for me to regret losing!'

WEEK SIX

On the first day of the sixth and final week of rehearsals, the technical crew were so behind with the lighting and effects for *Tell Me on a Sunday* that the *Variations* company rehearsal on stage was cancelled and they spent the afternoon in Studio 1 at Pineapple West. They worked on the Crazy Dance, the quintet to Variation 10, and the tap, especially the new section they had set on Saturday, improving, pointing up, polishing.

The one section Anthony wasn't happy about was Variation 22, the boys' dance just before the finale. The special effects he had in mind originally just weren't possible technically, and without them, it wasn't building to a climax in the way he had hoped, so he decided to make it a company dance instead, bringing in the girls.

Wayne felt it was the right decision. 'In terms of the story line, I couldn't see why I was joining in the boys' dance, or why the girls should go off, then come back on again later, and rejoin their partners, only to split up with them almost immediately. Now, they come back on together, and then split up, so it's very clear that what's happening is that they're all becoming individuals again.'

They were due back at the theatre for a dress run at seven, so while the others went for supper, Wayne and Anthony worked on the link between Wayne's trio with Andrea and Jane and the company dance that followed it. Instead of a walking pattern, it was now going to be a short solo for Wayne. 'It's an *adagio*, which means it's very slow, leisurely and graceful. A slow movement is more difficult than a quick one because you need far more control, and you mustn't use any force at all, so you have to be perfectly balanced and just sail round.'

They set it in no time at all. 'A bit of ballet!' Wayne exclaimed. 'They'll all say, "How deeply sensitive and artistic!", and it took us a mere five minutes to do!'

An hour later, back at the theatre, Wayne tried on his new costume for the first time, and was reasonably happy with it.

At a quarter to eight, they started the run-through. After the first double turn in his opening solo, Wayne suddenly stopped dancing. One of the spotlights was shining straight into his eyes, and it was, he said, like dancing blindfold. The light was adjusted, and they went back to the beginning, but half way through the tap duet, Wayne stopped again, walked off the stage, and came back moments later, minus his tap shoes, to talk to Anthony and John.

'I was very angry about the lack of light on the stage. We couldn't see where we were going, and it was very dangerous, so I said I wouldn't go on till they did something about it. I also found I couldn't spin in the centre of the stage because the groove for the wire that pulls Marti's gantry downstage runs straight through the middle – something I asked them to avoid right at the start.'

With additional light on stage, Wayne and Linda Brewer started the tap duet again, and this time, they went all the way through to the end. After some discussion, Wayne, Anthony and John Caird decided to change the opening. 'We felt it just wasn't strong

The tap duet is really coming together

enough as it was, so we decided to go back to the poster pose, with a flash of lightning projected on to the gauze screen. And while we're at it, we might as well go the whole hog, and light it in red and blue, like the poster, too.'

Tuesday got off to a bad start when a main fuse blew in the theatre, and the electricians took all morning to eliminate the resulting hum. The dancers were due to have their first run-through with the band, a day later than scheduled because the musicians had needed more time to master the score. Before they started, Wayne suggested that he and Linda Brewer ran through the tap on the spot so that the band could get the *tempo* right. In the meantime, Andrew Lloyd Webber had decided that he didn't want the piece to finish on a final, clean chord as they had rehearsed. Instead, he wanted it to finish, like the album, on a swooping cello *glissando*.

'It sounds great on the album, but I don't think it works theatrically. After forty-five minutes of dance, it's wrong to end with a downward swoop, and finish on a whimper. I didn't argue though, because Andrew had enough problems. It had become clear during the day that the band wasn't up to scratch. After all, *Variations* was composed for soloists, not for ordinary band musicians.'

Before they began the scheduled rehearsal of the song and rock'n'roll finale with Marti at five, Bob West wanted to work out the dancers' bows at the end of *Variations* – who would come on with whom, and in what order. That done, the stage had to be cleared ready for the first dress run of the whole show, due to start at eight.

Wayne's jacket of lights still wasn't ready, and he had had to change the taps on his shoes. 'Capezio taps sound great on wood, but on the surface we've got they just sound dead, so now we've both got jingle taps. They're harder to dance in because they're thicker, and more slippery, but there's no point in tapping your heart out if no one can hear you!'

Tell Me on a Sunday went very well, and the dancers all felt they had a good first half to follow. They began their run at half past nine, and all went well until half-way through the tap duet when the *tempo* was so wildly out that Wayne and Linda had no choice but to stop. The microphones, fixed under the stage to amplify the tapping, hadn't been switched through to Harry Rabinowitz's headphones, so he couldn't hear the dancers and couldn't gauge the *tempo*. A button was pressed so that he *could* hear, and they began again from the start of the tap duet. This time, the *tempo* was fine.

During the finale with Marti, Wayne didn't sing his first line of harmony and only joined in the rest of the song sporadically. 'I was just too exhausted after all that dancing!'

The following morning Wayne came in early to run through the *tempi* with the band. 'I also talked to Andrew about the ending, and he agreed to change it back to the way it was, with one, clean chord instead of the *glissando*. I think it's much better this way.'

After a photo session in costume for the press, the company changed back into rehearsal gear and went into the stalls bar for a song call. It had been decided after last night, that instead of singing his solo line of harmony, Wayne would sing the melody for the last two lines of the opening verse. 'I couldn't come straight in with the harmony because I had nothing to pitch it from, and I think, too, it sounded odd. This way means I'll have a bit of extra time to try and get some breath from somewhere – not that I'll be doing it anyway. From the way my wisdom tooth is playing up, I'll probably be in hospital having it out!'

(In fact, Wayne had the troublesome tooth out one Sunday in April and although his face was swollen and he was in great pain he didn't miss a single performance. But for the first few nights his dentist was standing by in the wings in case his stitches burst.)

The rest of the afternoon was devoted to a technical run, finalising the lighting, setting the computer that would project the slides on to the screen during Marti's half and Wayne's solo, and polishing the links.

In the dress run of *Variations* that night, all went well until Wayne almost tripped over the groove in the centre of the stage, and stopped, angry. After a brief, succinct discussion, a roll of

Wayne in performance – the opening Variation (top left) and his solo

The first full dress rehearsal in front of an invited audience – and the inquest afterwards

black gaffer tape was produced, and a strip placed over the length of the groove. They started again, and half way through the company tap, Wayne made his entrance in the long-awaited jacket of lights, though the lights weren't actually working. After a minute or two, while the company carried on tapping, he walked off stage, came back a moment later without the jacket and finished the run.

'It was too tight round the neck and across the chest so that I couldn't really move in it. And of course, the lights didn't work. That really annoys me – the jacket of lights was one of the first ideas we had, but they left it to the last minute and now there isn't time to get it working, so we'll have to scrap it without it really being tried.

'I'm still not happy about the amount of light on the stage, either. The light reflecting tape they put round the edge yesterday doesn't work, and you really can't dance flat-out if you're afraid you're going to fall off the front of the stage.'

When the dancers arrived on Thursday morning, a row of tiny red LEDs was being fixed to the front of the stage. After a lot of thought about the tap, Wayne, Anthony and John Caird decided to cut the part where Linda headed for the gantry, and replace it with them tapping round in a circle instead. They also decided to cut nine bars from Wayne's tap solo at the end. 'The music just went on repeating and repeating, and then, for no apparent reason, just stopped. By cutting it in half, we don't really lose anything.'

That evening's dress run was performed in front of an invited audience of friends, relatives and colleagues. They enjoyed *Tell Me on a Sunday*, but since most of them were dancers, it was *Variations* they had really come to see. They applauded the moment the curtain went up, appreciated every demonstration of skill, and even a minor mid-stage collision between Wayne and Linda Brewer in the new section of the tap didn't prevent them from cheering wildly at the end.

Even so, many of the dancers didn't feel their performances were as good as the previous night's and were rather despondent. But John Caird wasn't at all discouraged, and pointed out that they had another ten days before the press night to get it right. Wayne and Anthony disagreed. 'John was more concerned about the press reaction than we were. As far as we dancers were concerned, we had no more time. Our first performance was the following night; the audience had paid full price for their tickets, so they deserve a proper show!'

FIRST NIGHT...

Wayne left the theatre after the dress run on Thursday night, depressed and worried. 'I still had trouble seeing the edge of the stage, and, with the W-shaped cut-out, I was really concerned that I might fall off. But the biggest worry without a doubt was the music. Because the band had taken so long to master the score, we'd only had three runs with them, and the *tempi* were all over the place – the tap was too fast which was killing us, and my solo was too slow. Timing is *the* most critical thing in dance – if the *tempo* is too slow, you can't hold a jump in mid-air and wait for the band to catch up so you can land on the beat! It's important when you're singing, too, but at least then you can push ahead with the words and drag the band along with you. With dance, there's no way you can do that. If the band is playing too fast or too slow, all you can do is look hard at the conductor and hope he gets the message. But we can't even do that because Harry and the band are behind a curtain and he can only see us in long-shot on a tiny television monitor, so there is no way he can detect a significant look. If anything goes wrong, we'll just have to get on with it.'

Wayne got home just after eleven, too tired to go out for supper with friends as planned, and not really in the mood for company. Instead, he watched a video, and went to bed about two. 'I couldn't sleep because I was overtired, and the counts were going round and round in my head. Even if I'd had no other worries, they would have kept me awake because they're relentless. It's like being brainwashed! When I did finally fall asleep, I dreamt I had an ant living in a pore in the middle of my eyelid, and though I could see it wiggling about in a magnifying mirror, I just couldn't get it out!

'I woke around midday and crawled out of bed. I didn't really feel any different because it was the first performance that night. There is no feeling of excitement any more – I suppose I've been in the business too long for that! I knew all the dancers would give a performance, and I was reasonably happy with my own, PROVIDED we could get the *tempi* and the technical problems sorted out.'

The final dress rehearsal was due to start at two, but by the time Wayne arrived at the theatre around one, looking pale and strained, it had been postponed for an hour, and then soon after, was cancelled altogether. Everyone felt it was more important to spend the time working on the curtain calls and the rock'n'roll finale.

'There had been some disagreement about the *tempo* for my solo. Andrew wanted it played slower, but I knew from the way it had been choreographed, it had to be a beat faster than the band had played it last night. The music has to push me, drive me through the solo. It can't be slow. Finally, I said to Harry, "*You're* playing it, *I'm* dancing it – we must sort it out between us." In the end, Andrew agreed that it had been too slow, so that was that.'

They ran through the new section of the tap duet, where they had collided last night, and went over the *tempo* with the band several times until everyone was happy. But there were still problems with the tap – in spite of cutting the solo at the end in half the day before, Wayne still didn't feel it worked, so after discussing it with Anthony and John Caird, he decided to cut it altogether, and just dance off with the rest of the company instead.

'Had the jacket of lights worked out, there might have been some reason for keeping it in, but without that, there was no point. The music doesn't build, doesn't go anywhere – it just dies out, so I felt it was best if we just died out with it. In terms of the storyline, I feel it should have just ended with me being left alone on stage, suddenly realising that the others had gone, and then creeping off, slightly embarrassed. But as it is, with me coming back on, Linda following me and us doing the business with the towel, it's okay.'

The curtain calls and the rock'n'roll finale, everyone agreed, were a bit of a mess, so a number of changes were made. The dancers would stay on stage with Wayne after their bows, as Marti's gantry came downstage for the final song, instead of climbing on to it behind the screen as they had done, and Wayne and Marti would stay on the gantry for the first half of the rock'n'roll.

The company finished rehearsing at five, but Wayne carried on working, on the finale, on the tap and on his solo until after the stage should have been cleared, ready for the performance, at six-thirty.

At seven, he changed into his street clothes, went out and bought some Perrier water and a cheese-and-tomato sandwich – lunch AND tea! At half past seven, he began getting ready. 'I got dressed and put on my make-up, then when Marti went on stage at eight, I

started my warm-up. They've put up a *barre* in my dressing rooom, so I do an hour's ballet warm-up, which covers every muscle in your body.

'I think it's very important to get yourself out of breath before you go on stage, because otherwise it comes as such a shock to the system. I always do a few jumps to get me breathing hard, so that my lungs are open and working properly. People tend to forget that your lungs need warming up just as much as your muscles do. While I warmed up, I had the speaker on, so I could hear the audience really enjoying Marti's half. What with that and the fact that the band were playing better than I'd ever heard them, I thought it would probably be all right!'

At ten past nine, Wayne went down to the stage, during the interval, and did a few more exercises and jumps. 'I'm always very calm before I go on stage – totally under control with no sweaty palms, or thumping heart. Obviously, the adrenalin is going, but you have to learn to control it, so that you can dance in the way you want to. If you let yourself feel nervous, you won't dance as well. I don't have any pre-curtain rituals or superstitions. I'd be dead if I did! I'd go out there one night, realise that I hadn't done whatever it is, and think, "Oh God, I'm bound to fall over now!" and I would because if you *think* you're going to, you will!'

At twenty past nine, the curtain went up to reveal Wayne standing on stage, pointing skywards, and the audience applauded enthusiastically. 'It's nice to know, they're on your side, and it would be awful if they didn't clap, but some nights they won't and you have to be prepared for that. You can't rely on the audience to see you through. If no one applauds, or cheers or laughs, you still have to do the best you can.'

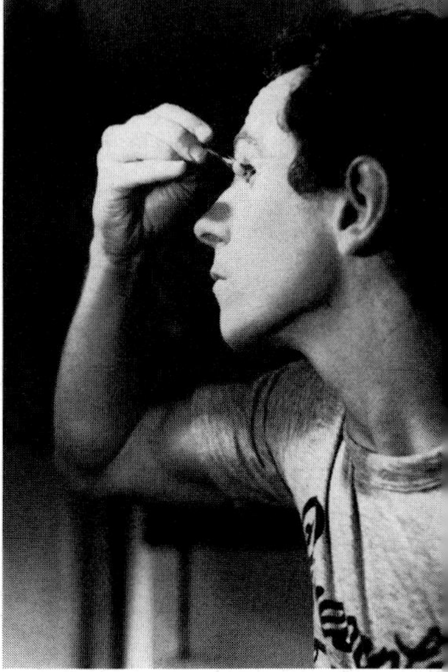

Opposite : The opening bars of Variations – *the movement builds from the hips to the feet to the shoulders, then the head*

Opposite and top: Wayne and Paul Tomkinson. Above and right: Wayne and Linda Gibbs

During the first week, Wayne acquires a red satin baseball cap for the tap

Opposite: The dancers in
performance and (below)
joined by Marti Webb for the
rock'n'roll finale

But they did all three in great measure – applauded and cheered the spectacular jumps and spins for which he is famous, and laughed at the flashes of Puckish humour – a cheeky wiggle here, a wicked grin there. As the band played the final chord, and the nine dancers stood on stage pointing skywards, the applause was ecstatic.

There were well deserved rounds of applause for each pair of dancers as they took their bows, but naturally Wayne got the loudest applause of all. But he took just one bow on his own, then insisted that the others join him.

As for the song, Wayne managed his solo melody line, but some of the high harmonies were too much for him to reach. 'To sing high quietly requires a lot of breath control, and after dancing flat out for forty-five minutes, I just didn't have any! If the song was a belter, I would have gone for it, but it's a gentle, romantic song, and I didn't want to ruin it by singing loud!'

The audience loved it, though, and gave the cast and the band a standing ovation. Andrew Lloyd Webber ran on to the stage to loud cheers, punching the air like a footballer who has just scored a winner which, in a sense, he had. He hugged Marti and Wayne, made a short speech of thanks, and called Anthony, John Caird, and Don Black, the lyricist, on stage to share in the acclaim, until the curtain finally came down.

Afterwards at a small drinks party in the stalls bar (the official first night party would be after the press night on 7 April), Wayne was tired, but reasonably happy. Even so his immediate response to the congratulations being heaped on him from all sides was, 'I nearly slipped on a drop of sweat during the solo. Did you notice?'

He was delighted by the audience's response, though also a bit surprised. 'It's quite something for a West End audience to sit through forty-five minutes of dance, without any dialogue or songs. It says a lot for the quality of the choreography, I think, and the talent of the dancers. Of course, I was relieved that it went off without a hitch, and that I didn't fall over, but I must admit the first thought that went through my head as we stood there taking the curtain calls was, How on earth am I going to get through *two* performances tomorrow?.'

...AND AFTER

Wayne got through both performances on Saturday without any difficulty, and during the next ten days, before the press night, standing ovations became the rule, rather than the exception.

The only changes made in this period were to the opening of the tap duet, and they were changes in style, not content. 'It wasn't really until we got into performing that the differences between Linda's opening music and mine really became clear. Hers is very tinselly, and she was playing it very dainty and coy. My music is funkier, more blasé, so I thought I'd play it that way, and *against* the way Linda was playing. And it seems to work very well.'

Although the critics were not meant to review the show before the press night, *The Sunday Times*'s Derek Jewell jumped the gun and published his review on 4 April. '. . . The magnificent Wayne Sleep and company, with choreography by Anthony van Laast to Andrew Lloyd Webber's 'Variations' showing an inspiration and originality London has almost never seen . . . an explosion of magic, a tonic to lift the heart . . . superb stuff. Run to it!'

Naturally everyone was delighted with the review, but old hands, like Wayne, tempered their pleasure with a degree of caution. 'The other critics won't like being pre-empted, and maybe they'll take it out on us. I'm already a bit apprehensive about the reviews, because I wonder who the papers will send. Most of them will send their drama critics, and this isn't drama – there is no text, no speeches, no acting of the kind they're used to, so quite what they'll make of it is anyone's guess!'

On press night, the curtain was due to go up an hour early at seven, and Wayne got to the theatre just before six, exhausted, having spent the day dashing round London, buying presents for all the cast. 'By the time I got to the theatre, I was so tired I had to put my feet up for half an hour and then I realised that I was starving hungry, so I had to rush down Shaftesbury Avenue, and get myself a McDonald's. The audience was already arriving at that time, so God knows what they thought when they saw me dashing out of the stage door – probably that I'd changed my mind about the whole thing!'

The curtain went up just after seven, and *Tell Me on a Sunday* was greeted with enthusiasm. Then *Variations* began and from the moment the curtain went up it was clear that the audience loved it. Every comic nuance got a huge laugh, every piece of virtuosity was greeted with loud cheers and when the final chord was struck, the audience leapt to its feet in the wildest ovation yet. They loved the rock'n'roll finale, too, and the company took four curtain calls. They could have taken more, but as Wayne said, they didn't want to milk it!

The first night party was held at the nearby L'Escargot restaurant in Soho, with a splendid sit-down supper upstairs and a non-stop disco downstairs. 'I don't normally like parties much, but it was lovely. Everyone was genuinely delighted with the way it had gone, and Andrew was even talking about the possibility of an American production next year. The only problem I had was getting through the evening relatively sober. I couldn't risk drinking too much, not with a show the next day.'

Wayne left the party, still in full swing, about half past one, and didn't wait up for the first editions of the papers.

The reviews fell into four categories. Two reviewers hated the whole show and couldn't find a single good word to say for it. The second group shared the view expressed by *The Spectator*'s critic. 'Most people including me, would still prefer a musical with characters and a story, but "Dance" is a triumph, and promises more for the future.'

A third group weren't too keen on the first half, but loved the second, while the rest of the reviews ranged from very good to raves. *The Observer*'s Robert Cushman wrote '. . . the music combines with the dancing of Wayne Sleep and his acrobatic cohorts to jolt us out of our seats, Anthony van Laast's choreography is fiery and funny, its execution more so. Those of us who don't normally get to see much ballet were exhilarated and relieved to find our enthusiasm shared by the buffs.'

Irving Wardle, of *The Times*, also loved it, though he kept referring to Wayne Sleep and *three* couples or *six* dancers, so Nicholas Dromgoole, *The Sunday Telegraph*'s dance critic, started his review by setting the record straight. 'There are nine dancers, NINE dancers, dancers who can actually dance, well-trained dancers, dancers with talent, dancers who are exciting to watch . . . Anyone who thinks I was harsh about the dance in *Cats* should compare it to Anthony van Laast's choreography for *Song and Dance*, and I hope they will see what I mean . . . Of course, there is only one Wayne Sleep, and it is his blazing talent, his irrepressible sense of fun and joy in dance as a performance that underpins the whole event . . . It could be a milestone. It has to be seen.'

Nobody could fail to be delighted by a review like that, particularly from a specialist in the field, but for Wayne the pleasure was slightly diminished by the viciousness of a few reviews, and by the fact that some critics simply didn't grasp that the dancers were playing characters and not simply being themselves. 'A couple of reviews said I looked smug, or self-congratulatory, so it was hard to warm to me. But it wasn't me – it was my character! They wouldn't assume an actor was simply being himself, would they? But that was the problem – most of them weren't dance critics, and don't really understand dance. On the most basic level, one critic wrote about my clichéd, old *fouettés en tournant* at the end. Well, they're not *fouettés*, they're clichéd, old multiple turns *à la seconde*! But to be honest, the reviews didn't really matter that much. We knew from the response of the audiences that we had a good show.'

Looking back over the whole project, Wayne felt that the show had changed quite a lot from the original concept in the course of the creative process. 'To a large extent, the storyline has gone. Having it there while we worked was helpful because it gave us a skeleton on which to hang the flesh, but once it began to get in the way, it had to go. The story is still there – just – and if the audience wants to see it, they can. But the piece doesn't rely on it, and people can see it simply as an exciting piece of dance. And one of the major achievements, I think, is that it *is* a piece – it doesn't look like twenty-three separate variations.

'Overall, what I hoped *Variations* would do is provide a vehicle for some of the very exciting dance talent we have in this country, and prove that it is possible to put on a West End show with dancing of the same standard as you see at the Royal Opera House which the public would really enjoy. From the response we get out there night after night, it would seem that we've done it!'

Gay Search,

who worked with Wayne Sleep on this book, is a freelance writer and broadcaster who has contributed to many newspapers and magazines, like *Radio Times*, *Good Housekeeping* and *Woman's Journal*. She has written a number of books, including *Divorce and After*, in conjunction with Anglia Television's series of the same name, and *The Down Your Way Book*. She is a frequent member of Radio 4's popular 'News Quiz' team and has recently presented two television series, 'Couples' for BBC 1 and 'Minus One' for Tyne Tees. She is married and lives in London.

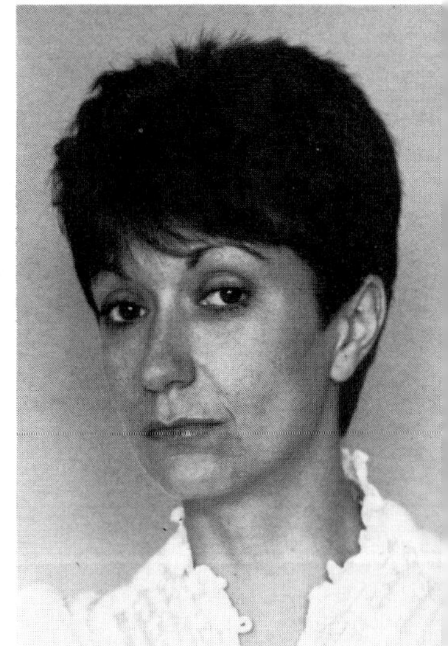